Amateur Passions

LOVE STORIES?

Lorna Tracy

Virago
London

Published by VIRAGO PRESS Limited 1981
Ely House, 37 Dover Street,
London W1X 4HS

Copyright © Lorna Tracy, 1973, 1974, 1975,
1977, 1978, 1981

Typeset by Elanders Limited and
printed by Lowe and Brydone Limited
of Thetford, Norfolk

Contents

Talking About It · 7

The Terry Cloth Mother · 27

Threadball · 47

The Mama Stories:
    Bridger's Moth · 61
    Wool · 75
    The Persistence of Rathbun · 98

While Nancy Listened On The Bed · 125

The Holy Act of Water Contemplation · 153

The Spoilers · 167

Acknowledgments

The author is grateful to Northern Arts and to The Arts Council of Great Britain for financial assistance in preparing this manuscript.

Some of these stories originally appeared in New Stories 1 & 2 (The Arts Council of Great Britain); Introduction 5 (Faber & Faber); Bananas; Proteus; Hecate and Stand.

Talking
About It

'Do you run around your apartment in New York in an undraped state like you do here?' That's what my father wanted to know as I slapped past him yesterday on rubber shower shoes – all I ever seem to want to wear in summer. He was stretched out on the living room couch. Newly retired and not long out of the coronary ward.

'Yes,' I said. 'Lots.'

'That's not a very good idea, with all those men around to get aroused.'

'There aren't any men in my apartment,' I said.

My father had been turning water out of the irrigation ditch on to our lawn. Now he was resting while he waited for the yard to flood. He elaborately avoided looking at me.

A day or two before my mother, in an unwonted burst of confidentiality, had confessed to me that she thought the male body was the ugliest thing in the world, so I'd asked her whether God hadn't created man in His own image.

'No one knows what God looks like,' had been her answer to that.

'Why, like us,' I'd said. 'Isn't that what the Scriptures say?'

'The Scriptures mean the *spiritual* image of God,' she'd said, as if to a child. 'Only in babies is the male body the slightest bit attractive.' So I'd said it was the same body, infant or adult.

'Lots of changes take place,' she'd replied.

'Not fundamentally.'

'Well, I firmly believe in keeping it covered up.'

When we are children we are forced to comply with inexplicable codes of conduct. When we grow up we often discover it is easier to do what others tell us. In the end we usually prefer to be betrayed by someone else rather than betray ourselves. I've always gone back home for my summer vacation. I don't know what draws me there. Habit, probably. For a month of bright mornings I lie in the little bedroom of my childhood just behind the kitchen and I can still hear my parents talking at breakfast exactly as they talked during the war, when the two things invariably discussed in the third person singular, feminine gender, were the Axis and me. The difference now is that I have the third person singular, feminine gender pretty much to myself. The Axis doesn't come into it any more.

This morning I heard my mother say to my father: 'Don't you think we ought to take Simba out to the vet's today and have him put to sleep? It will have to be done before long anyway, and tomorrow we're all leaving on the trip.'

'You haven't said anything about it to her, have you?'

'Oh, no.'

'Well, don't. It would just upset her.'

He's right, clever old Dad. Their plot against my pet cat shocks me to the marrow. And once again as so often in the past I'm at least grateful to have overheard the plan so that I don't have to respond to it for the first time in their presence, because my response is to cry and I never cry in front of my parents.

Every child resorts to eavesdropping sometimes as the only way to find out what adults really are thinking, what they actually intend to do. I don't think my parents ever suspected how early I woke up as a child or how much I was able to hear through the kitchen wall. When my father would thump on my door just before he went off to his job and shout: 'Time to get up, girl!' I always appeared to be fathoms deep in sleep. I knew that ten minutes later my mother was going to come in, pull back all the blankets and chirp at me to wake up and hear the birdies sing! She always said that, even when there wasn't a bird to be heard in the whole state of Wyoming.

By the time I was old enough for school my mother hadn't much more to do in life than keep our tiny house and attend to my moral development. With both these stewardships she struggled constantly and never had the satisfaction of seeing the effect of her labours last more than ten minutes. But of course I knew it was wrong to eavesdrop. What I also knew was that nothing of any consequence was going to be said in my presence. From wake-up-and-hear-the-birdies-sing to now-I-lay-me-down time all I could hope to hear were either cheerful banalities or else orders phrased as questions about the time: 'Isn't it time to get up? Isn't it time to leave for school? Time to wash the dishes, time to finish your homework, time to go to bed?' Apparently my parents spoke candidly only very early in the morning. They had a routine. While my mother was squeezing the orange juice, cooking Cream O' Wheat, making coffee and burning slices of bread in the oven because we couldn't afford an electric toaster, my father would read to her the day's lesson from a church booklet, followed by the recommended verses from the Bible. Then they would get down to the interesting things, which often included some frank talk about friends, relatives or me. They must have believed it would set me a bad example if I ever heard anything but good spoken of others, or any good at all spoken of myself. I held my breath and listened to every word. Eavesdropping might be wrong but the morning came when it saved me from a crime even worse than itself. Without eavesdropping I never could have known in time about my parents' intention to give me a gold locket on my eleventh birthday. This vital intelligence came the very morning after I had stolen a locket from my best friend. For weeks, for months, I'd coveted a locket of Donna Jean Pickett's. It was like a miniature book on a fine chain. Inside the gold and enamelled covers were several hinged leaves containing tiny photographs in oval frames. But I had not thought of stealing it until after my mother told me *never* to beg her again for a locket of my own. She had said in a voice that made it quite clear my cause was hopeless: 'Gold lockets are much too expensive for plasterers' daughters.' Donna Jean was not a plasterer's daughter; her father owned the big smelly meat-packing plant out on the edge of town that had a railway siding named after it, so that you could see PICKETT spelled out loud and clear on a sign beside the tracks whenever you drove by. There were objects on her mother's dressing table that had never even been in my mother's wildest dreams: crystal bottles with crystal stoppers shaped like frozen flames, and atomisers (I learned the word from Donna Jean) that produced the smell of roses, and something even better, when you squeezed the netted rubber bulbs.

In my lust for the book-shaped locket I hadn't taken into account the reasons why I would derive no pleasure from possessing it. I didn't dare wear it, for one thing, and for another I was afraid to go play any more with Donna Jean because I was sure she knew what I had done, even though I had carried out my theft with the utmost cunning at a time when two or three other girls were also playing dress-up at her house. 'I thought I'd lost mine,' Donna Jean told me on my birthday when I showed her my heart-shaped locket. 'It was really funny. I looked all around in my jewel box and I couldn't find it, you know. And it was really funny, the very next day my mother told me to go look again and it was right there on the top. Mommy thinks someone "borrowed" it.' I had listened to this steaming with shame. I stood before my best friend a barely redeemed thief and the sin of eavesdropping had been the instrument of my redemption. I was morally in great confusion. Had I kept Donna Jean's locket even one day longer I would surely have been confronted by her terrifying mother and forced to confess. Then I would have been sent home with orders to confess all over again to my own mother. My father would have whipped me with his razor strop when he got home, and I'd never have been given a locket of my own after all. I wanted to avoid the fact that my mother had broken her word to me. She had promised not to give me a locket and then she had given me one. So the way I looked at it in the end was that for all their righteousness my parents had been systematically stealing from me for years. What they had been stealing was my free time. Bedtime for me had been arbitrarily fixed at eight-thirty, regardless of the season, the day of the week, the position of the sun in the sky, or the hour when anyone else my age was summoned in from play. My mother believed that a person got his best sleep before midnight. It was a lunatic thing to believe, and even if it hadn't been applied to me I would have objected to it on principle. I didn't know which made me angrier, my affronted common sense or my infringed personal freedom. This chronological nonsense was particularly intolerable in the summer, when school was out and the hot, still evenings lasted so long and were so richly lighted. Sneaking, climbing, racing, hiding, seeking had an edge to them then that they lacked at all other times. The grass was just on the point of turning slippery and cool and fragrant and all my friends still had at least another half hour to play when sharp at eight-thirty my parents would appear to fetch me home, and there was nothing I could do about it except not go quietly. The neighbourhood rang with my furious shrieks while my parents, pinching my arms painfully between them, told me how ashamed of me they were as they dragged me off to bed.

I would sit in the blue twilight of my hot little bedroom, the shirt of my seersucker pyjamas defiantly unbuttoned all the way down, staring furiously through the window screen into the savannah shadows of the stag-horn sumac under which my cat Simba stalked herds of insect antelope. Even a pet cat had more freedom than I. Now and then the motionless air would freight a shout across from my friends still playing on the other side of the block. At the sound of them my smouldering rage would simply blaze up. I'd pull the sheets off my bed, intending to knot them together and escape through the window, but the thick cotton was too much for my small hands. Eventually I would cry myself into an exhausted sleep. In the revengeful dreams that seared my eyelids I would stand with my heel on my father's neck and feel my mother's bare face under my naked foot, sovereign at last in the kingdom of Angry Dreams. When I woke in the morning there was always a blanket over me.

I never did escape from home through a window. I finally just went away to college. Even there institutional authority *in loco parentis* punished me with dorm hours. And now for several years I've lived alone in Manhattan where there is no one to care whether I ever come in at night at all.

I'm still young enough to be able to obliterate the evidence of weeping by applying cold water to my face. After I've done this I go into the kitchen to make myself some coffee. Almost at once my father strolls in. The kitchen is not his natural habitat and he doesn't know what to do with himself there if he's not eating a meal. He stacks one plate on another and shoves them to the back of the counter and says: 'Don't you think we ought to do something to help Simba into the Happy Hunting Ground?'

'I don't know,' I say. 'Why should we?'

The reply comes from my mother in the living room, where she is dusting table tops and monitoring my reactions: 'He's been sick so much lately, Elinor. Those hairballs of his. And it's not just that. He's getting too old to protect himself anymore from the dogs. They're so bad around here now. You don't know. We're all going away for two weeks and if the dogs ever got him, why they'd just tear him to pieces.' She appears at the kitchen door with her big knotted hands twisted in her bib apron. 'No, Elinor, the time has come to have him put to sleep.'

'Okay.'

'Well, it's the merciful thing to do, Elinor.' She's wringing the apron so hard that the dust spurts out of it. 'Dad and I thought we'd take him to the vet's this morning. We don't like to do it but he's old and sick and there are so many dogs in the neighbourhood now. I've had to rescue him from them twice just in the last few weeks when they've had him cornered on the porch.'

'We'll all be going away tomorrow,' says my father, 'so this is really the time to take care of him.'

Together they closed in on me: 'The neighbours would feed him while we're gone, of course, but they can't be expected to keep him safe from the dogs.'

'Not when they own the dogs!' adds my father, who always wants things to be joky if they possibly can be.

'Okay,' I repeat in an absolutely neutral voice. My father asks me if I want to go to the vet's with them. I'm looking at the morning paper, pretending to read the news. I tell him no.

'I'll just vacuum in here and then we'll go,' says my mother. My father wants to put Simba in a box. My mother wants to carry him in a blanket. My father says he will get away from her and jump out the car window. My mother says they can roll the windows up. My father remains in the kitchen. He is certainly baffled by my indifference. Probably he is wondering whether city life has calloused me or whether he ought to commend me for displaying – I imagine him sorting through his Handbook of Suitable Phrases for Family Occasions – 'a fine new maturity in accepting the proper bedtime for your cat.' Certainly I have never simply accepted anything before. 'Life is just *full* of things we don't like,' my mother would regularly declare while I was growing up objecting to everything that befell me, 'but that doesn't mean you can have a tantrum every time something goes wrong.' Talk like that only made me the angrier, something she never seemed to grasp. My mother is one sort of Thurber woman, one of the homely, befuddled sort, absorbed in hearing seals bark, cleaning under radiators and 'getting at' things. There is a puzzled expression in her face under all the flustered busyness there. Her handsome legs disappear into 'sensible' shoes as sturdy as a logger's boots. Her stockings somehow always wrinkle into long thin diagonal blisters. Her profile looks drawn by a blind hand that can scarcely relate the lips to the chin and the nose to the lips. I go on pretending to read the newspaper, hoping my father will not try to say anything about the 'improvement' in my behaviour. I'm aware of it as of a tumour somewhere between my ribs. A greyish, possibly heart-shaped lump that interferes a little with my breathing. Malignant maturity. Irreversible. Terminal.

We've had Simba for seventeen years. He was my eighth birthday present, a tottery kitten. If he were a human being he'd be eighty-five years old, if what they say is true, that one year in a cat's life is equal to five in a person's. I don't know that it is, but that's what I've heard. Anyway, a seventeen-year-old cat is a very old cat. The difficult thing is that he hasn't grown old in a recognisably human way. I don't know whether, if he had, what was now proposed would seem acceptable. But animals age from the inside out and my cat seems unchanged. He is in his dotage as he was in his prime – asleep. But cats *do* sleep. They sleep so much my father used to wonder why they don't get bedsores.

Scenes from his life as a kitten come back to me. The afternoon he spent sitting in the bathtub intently looking up at the drops forming on the rim of the faucet, then peering with cocked head into the mystery of the plug-hole, the mystery of life. The pattern of smeared pad-marks on the bottom of the tub showed he'd tried to get out and couldn't. Joyfully I had 'rescued' him from his enamelled cast-iron trap and imagined that he was grateful. I'd been so proud of him, his great size (mostly a hairy illusion of size); his magnificent Persian coat that gave him such awful hairballs. Visitors always fussed over him in a satisfying way, although he never solicited their admiration but withdrew to stare at them from under-neath the couch until they went away. The only callers he ever took an interest in were the very few we had who hated cats. Then he would lean drunk with pleasure against their shifty ankles and make love to their shoes and if any dared to sit down he would throw himself upon them and try to thrust his head into their oxters. Such a perverse response to visitors appealed to me. I wished that I dared to take a similarly independent attitude myself instead of always being 'such a nice little girl'. But there were other times when I'd hold Simba in my arms and stand at the back door next to where the basement steps went down into the dark and I would see how easily I could throw him down those stairs, throw him down them hard. And then I would imagine the hurt thing crawling away to hide itself and I would feel such pity and remorse that I could scarcely bear it. Even so, the thought would return again and again to torment me. I wanted to give my kitten whipped cream; I wanted to throw him down the stairs. Perhaps it was a strain of the same desire that had made my father as a boy long to stand up in the classroom and claim every misdemeanour the schoolmarm inquired about when he had not committed any of them. The innocent boy who *feels* guilty. A congenitally bad conscience seeks its reason.

My brother, who gets up even later than I do when he's home, has come into the kitchen and now without even watching I know that my father has reached up awkwardly to swat his son on the shoulder. 'Well, well, well! How's the architect this morning?'

'Just fine, Dad. Good morning, Elinor.'

'Morning,' I mutter, keeping my head in the paper. I still haven't taken in a single item of the day's news.

The minute she hears Ned's voice my mother rushes into the kitchen to cook his breakfast. 'Now then, Ned, you can have anything that you want – bacon and eggs, pancakes, French toast. There's a little steak. There's some nice cold orange juice in the refrigerator. I squeezed it fresh this morning. My, *my*, Dad and I are glad to have you home! And Elinor too.'

They always treat Ned like an honoured guest. I suppose it's because he comes home so seldom. He'd been pleased to sneak off and join the Air Force before he'd even finished high school, leaving me to grow up all alone being called 'she' while he was always Ned. 'We got a letter from Ned today,' my mother would carol out on certain days as soon as my father came in from work. 'Ned's going to be stationed in Texas.' 'Ned's learning to fly in a Link trainer.' 'Ned's sent us a snapshot.' Ned, Ned, Ned. Next week he's going to marry a nurse back in Omaha and we're driving there with him for the wedding. In a way it's because of Ned that Simba's going to be 'put to sleep' today. It isn't fair to blame Ned, but I blame him anyway.

My father sits down at the kitchen table. Except for being about a foot taller and considerably younger, Ned looks just like him. They each wear a pale toothbrush moustache over the perpendicular upper lip, whose long vertical drop is abruptly arrested at the protruding of the pink and glistening lower lip. In both of them the smoothness and moistness and meatiness of this forms the sharpest contrast to the dry hairy moustache. In Ned that lower lip not only juts forward but drops a little open, as though he were constantly absorbed in deep thoughts. It gives him an appearance of stuporous concentration which I consider fraudulent. While Ned drinks his iced orange juice and eats his little steak my father risks a serious conversation with him. He can do this because Ned stays calm. If an argument seems to be coming Ned disappears. He just goes away. The doctor's ordered my father not to fight, argue or run. Since any subject is arguable if I'm there to argue it, conversations never even get started between us now. 'We won't discuss it,' he says as soon as anything comes up. The weather isn't even a safe subject. Any reference to the temperature leads sooner or later to the setting of the thermostat. My father believes in the Lord God Jehovah and the seventy-two degree comfort zone. I break out in goose-flesh at seventy-two degrees. My mother is sometimes warm and sometimes cold at seventy-two degrees. Ned, naturally, feels neither hot nor cold at any temperature. Which is why I'm surprised now to hear him defending Frank Lloyd Wright with what for Ned is some vehemence. He explains to my father how 'Mr Wright' as Ned calls him always follows principle, not precedent, in his designs; grounds his work on natural forms; designs buildings organically from the inside out; wants to produce a true and ideal American house for Americans in the lower income brackets, and insists that young architects be trained to do the same, never mistaking the part for the whole, recognizing that all art is a unity, serviceable to man's higher ideal of himself. Ned becomes quite oratorically scornful as he says: '"Safety first" is a banker's motto. Mr Wright says tell the bankers to reform!'

My father the plasterer, who says he knows something about the construction business, doesn't see how any of Wright's ideas can be other than impractical, wasteful and expensive.

'Then so is the human spirit,' says Ned.

I'm longing to say how Wright's ideas excite me, how they correspond to my own sense of the deformities of contemporary life. I want to tell Ned how the city I live in constantly rubs me raw in the abrasive channels of its streets and then pours its ceaseless noise, like salt, into the wounds so that it is healing to come back to this poky little one-storey town in the hills. But I have never said this to anyone. I pretend to like the city. And I have been pretending not to listen to my brother for so long that I can't give myself away now.

My mother wants to know: 'Hasn't Frank Lloyd Wright been divorced?' Any man who has been divorced isn't fit to hold opinions on art, truth, or the state of the nation's building trade.

My father gets up from the table. 'Come on, Mother. We'd better go to the vet's.'

She disappears into the basement to look for something to wrap the cat in. I set my coffee cup in the sink and slip out to the garage to look for Simba. He's lying asleep in the sun on a ragged Navajo blanket folded across the end of my father's work bench. When he hears someone coming he focuses his ears, sits up just far enough to brace himself with his forelegs and yawns enormously. In the delicate groove of his mouth his glistening tongue curls like Christmas ribbon. I touch his white coat, hot, and soft as feathers. 'They're going to kill you today, kitty.' He smiles austerely, flickering his tail just at the tip. His green eyes divide down the middle. He stares at me through the thin black spars as through a crack in a door. I remember the other time he went to the vet's, when he was hardly more than a kitten. 'It's to have an operation,' my mother had explained by way of not explaining. I hadn't really supposed it was any use to ask what the operation was for but I asked anyway. 'It's to make him a nice pet,' she'd said. Where would the operation be? 'You'll see when he gets home.' But when he got home I couldn't see the smallest sign. I'd had a notion it would have to do with that little pink thorny thing that he could pull out to wash but that was still there. So after some experimenting with spellings I found a word in the dictionary that I had overheard my father using recently at breakfast: *castrate* (kas'trāt) *vt*. To deprive of the testicles. How like a dictionary to define one big word with another. So I looked up 'testicle' and found out that it was a male 'genital' gland and I looked up 'genital' and there at last I confronted the awful word 'sex'. In the end all it seemed Simba had been deprived of was something under his tail that his long hair covered up anyway. It would be a long time before I fully understood what Simba had lost through his operation and why the loss had made him 'a nice pet' but at least I knew better than to speak of castration in the presence of grown-ups so I'd learned something of importance. And once again, learned it through eavesdropping.

Simba lies back again on his blanket, leaving one foreleg stretched out lion-style, weighty with poise, filling the minimum space for his mass. I stroke the short hairs on his flat Persian nose, and move my finger across the cool pink tip with its special moist surface. He draws his head away and out from under silk tufts on his paw come hooks. 'Please don't mind, kitty. I just want to remember you.' Behind the long hairs screening the entrance to his ears are glossy pink pillars and sculptings sensitive to the vibrations of a world I can't know anything about. I put my hand against his side and seem to feel the purr that no one has ever been able to hear. I wonder in what sense I can really think of him as 'my' cat. He's never had any need of me.

I can hear my mother's footsteps on the basement stairs

now. It occurs to me she'll probably come straight out here to the garage and find me talking to my cat, whose death sentence I still might commute for a time if I were to make enough of a scene. I stroll out into the street and re-enter the house through the front door, as if I'd been off somewhere down the road, not giving my cat a thought. I begin to wash the breakfast dishes. Not just my own but everyone's. I haven't washed dishes since I've been home. My mother comes into the kitchen carrying an old flannel sheet that I'd always wrapped Simba in after giving him one of the baths my mother regularly decreed he must have because he possessed the potential for perfect whiteness.

'What's the sheet for?'

'To carry the cat in.'

'You'll just scare him if you put him in that. He'll think you're going to give him a bath.'

'I've got to wrap him up. He'll scratch me if I don't.'

'Sure he'll scratch you if you come at him with *that*.'

'No, Elinor. He hates riding in the car. If he's not wrapped up he'll scratch me and get away.'

'Have you located the victim yet?'

'No. I'm just going to look for him now. I suppose he's run away.'

'I should think so. What's the difference whether you save him from the neighbours' dogs if you deliver him to the vet in a sheet?'

'You're so cruel, Elinor.'

'What are you going to tell him? Are you going to tell him about heaven?'

'Oh, Elinor, don't talk like that.'

But I want to intensify her unhappiness. 'Will you get another cat?'

'Oh, no.'

'More economising?' Half my college education had been bought with my mother's sacrifices.

'Oh, Elinor, you just seem to *enjoy* hurting people. I don't understand it, why you should want to be like that.

So insensitive.' Her voice goes high and thin. Another minute she'll be crying openly. 'If you don't care about your mother's feelings you might at least think of your dad's. He wore his heart out working for you.'

The window over the sink looks out on to the sunny lawn. I remember how Simba has always seemed to enjoy it out there – bird-watcher, stalker of bugs, the whole of him moving like a single eye, his plans twitching in his tail. I'm sorry that in a way all I ever did for him was to give him the baths he hated so much, and then laughed at him when he was all wet because he resembled a scale model dinosaur skeleton with the pride of his tail dragging like a dripping stick behind his ridiculously long hind feet. But I laugh again just to think of it. I'd bring him up into the kitchen to dry, and he'd stay all day in front of the hot-air register huddled on a rag rug, licking his soaked hair into thick spikes and shivering and turning and turning dolefully around on the rug, shaking one leg and then another. It took the whole day for him to dry but then, how splendid he was with his great tail once more upright and following him everywhere like a pillar of cloud. He was the admiration of the neighbourhood. People slowed down in their cars to get a better look at him on the porch.

There used to be a grove of elms and cottonwoods you could see from the kitchen window, too, but that's gone now and a one-storey pre-stressed concrete extension of the grade school is spread where scuffed roots had sheltered my wartime fantasies of mountain combat and covered wagons. I look at that concrete and think of the lake in lower Central Park with its sick grey skin and then I remember the first time I ever saw the Guggenheim Museum like a seashell among the shoeboxes of Fifth Avenue – womanly, modest, radiant, rhythmic, wearing no more than three concentric bands of natural shadow. I'd been told Wright's design was 'ugly', but it is the rest of the city that seems ugly to me. To me that skyline in the daytime looks about as beautiful as a sawbones' bagful of hypodermics needling the bruised sky.

To me Manhattan is a cemetery for monsters and I never pass a day there without thinking of what my mother always told me when we'd go to decorate the family graves: 'Never walk on a grave,' she'd say. 'It pinches the person.' In Manhattan the taste of my own blood is ever in my mouth.

I'm a secretary for a brokerage firm on Park Avenue. There's something in the atmosphere of the place that's like insecticide on an orchard. The apples are all huge and shiny and unblemished. No worms feed there, but no birds sing, either. It is rich with the sterility of money reproducing itself. There is no life in it. The men, the executives, the brokers themselves, all seem half-paralyzed. My boss, Mr Cornish, appears almost afraid to speak to me. I feel he would prefer it if I didn't have to arrive in the morning the way he did, on an elevator, but could simply be there when he came in, like the IBM machines, our works cased in thin steel cladding of some neutral shade. He would prefer to touch that by accident to touching anyone's warm flesh. He seems almost as uneasy in the company of his colleagues as he is with the girls who type his letters. Do his responsibilities weigh so heavily upon him? Does language, except when used to speak of stocks and bonds, come so near to unnerving him? When he dictates to me his words rush out but he also constantly interrupts himself. Uh ... uh ... uh. He is always caught in the tail of my eye, just passing to one side of my desk, a shape with high hunched shoulders and the left hand hidden in the pocket of his coat.

Manhattan of the tombstones and the zombies. I wasn't even surprised to discover that its plane trees are man-made, designed by botanists crossing things.

Apart from the Guggenheim I can remember only one other creature there who was so natural it stopped me in my tracks – a young black boy walking in the contracted shadows of late morning in the summer of West 101st Street. He seemed both gnomon and shadow, Time itself out for a walk in the sun, infinitely young and pert. His shaved skull, the perfect curves of his cranial bones worked in tiny spirals of black wool on brown silk with smooth perfect crescents cut out over the ears; short straight slender nose; carved full lips, large white eyes with dark liquid centres, the curve back of his lashes, the curve of his forehead. I was wild with admiration. He was like a piece of the very rarest art, both ceremonial and beyond ceremony. His face was without expression, or the expression concentrated inwardly upon some – some what? Some dream of brown girls? Some ball game? A rumble? I could hardly bear to think of that superb head not safe behind silk ropes and bulletproof glass but carried recklessly along West 101st Street on the shoulders of a mortal boy, constantly at risk.

When my parents come back from the vet's carrying the folded flannel sheet I ask them if they had stayed to watch the execution.

'No, of course not,' says my mother.

Ned wants to know if they gave Simba extreme unction. My mother smiles a little, clearly not wanting to, and says she doesn't think he was a Catholic.

'Maybe not,' says my father, 'but he sure was a cat'lick, wasn't he?' Joky old Dad.

Ned says: 'Well, it's never too late, you know!' His fiancée is a Catholic. He says she's supposed to pray every day for his conversion, right up to the hour of her death if he should prove so obstinate.

'It was a sad errand but it was for the best,' says my mother, ready to repeat the litany of the dangerous world. 'We've done the right thing, the merciful thing.'

She goes to the basement to put away the sheet and I return to the garage, taking in this time how dusty the place is. Whenever I had been punished as a child I had always come out here afterwards to snuggle my cat and tell him where I intended to go when I ran away from home that night, taking him with me, and he had always listened quite patiently as long as I didn't cry on him. He hated even a single drop of water. The rest of us, each in his own way, had done something similar. My father would scratch Simba's ears and talk to him in a funny high voice that was a kind of verbal stroking; my mother would give him something extra to eat. Even Ned occasionally told him that he was 'a funny old cat'. Much more than an ornamental family pet Simba was as near being the centre of affectionate exchange as anything our family had and now I want to understand our tolerance for his death. I want to relate it to something more profound than casual murder, but it can't be related to anything more profound. Everything else has got to be related to *it*.

Something seems to brush past my brain like a bat's wing in the dark. I stare out at the empty lawn through the unwashed window smeared with webs and the dangling husks of moths and the sunlit grass blurs. I wait, sighing to force back the flood sensation. After I can breathe again I can see quite clearly that the shadows on the lawn are so sharp they would cut off my feet if I stepped among them.

In the living room my brother is reading to my father from a magazine article on Frank Lloyd Wright. Something he reads makes them laugh. I laugh too, although I haven't heard what the joke is. As Kahlil Gibran might have said if he'd thought of it, what is laughter but another kind of weeping?

The
Terry Cloth
Mother

PART ONE · An Omen

Gail Schwartzendruber had not evened the corners of the bedsheet after she had hauled it out of the automatic washing machine

A QUARTER A LOAD

POSITIVELY NO DYEING

in her apartment-house basement at the conclusion of the damp-dry cycle, so that when she folded the sheet part of the hem on the yellow side hung down several inches below the hem on the white side. That's when Gail Schwartzendruber first noticed that there *was* a white side.

WHITER THAN WHITE!

WHITE AS NEW!

One side of the sheet was sweat-yellow. It had been sweat-yellow for years. But, until now, so had the other side. Both sides of the whole bedsheet had been sweat-yellow for years.

'Well, it can't have been the soap,' said Gail Schwart-zendruber to the QUARTER A LOAD sign. She always washed both sides of her bedsheets in the same soap and water. She was a clean girl, not a meticulous one. The same water would do for both sides of a thing. It was a matter of thrift, really. Gail Schwartzendruber was a thrifty girl. Laboratory technicians had to be thrifty and they had to be girls. 'You young ladies have superior manual dexterity,' said the Hospital Personnel Director to female applicants with science degrees, forgetting for the moment about Rubinstein and Menuhin. Even, apparently, forgetting about those teams and teams of male surgeons. Moreover there was something else about that bedsheet. In three places on the hem of the white side was written the word 'REPENT'.

'This just isn't my bedsheet,' said Gail Schwartzendruber to her blue plastic laundry basket. 'I guess I must have unloaded the wrong machine.' However reasonable her hypothesis seemed at first it did not stand up under rigorous examination. Rigorous examination of alternative automatic washing machines in the laundry room of her apartment-house basement proved beyond dispute that there were none. The laundry room of her apartment-house basement contained just one automatic washing machine – the machine that had offered Gail Schwartzen-druber this sweat-yellow bedsheet having one white side.

And in at least three places on the hem of the white side was written the word 'REPENT'.

'You see,' said Gail Schwartzendruber to the automatic washing machine, 'I know this isn't my sheet because nothing has been written on my sheets since my mother sent me away for a week to Camp Alice Organdorf on July 16, 1949. Even then, my sheets did not say "REPENT". They said "Gail Marie Schwartzendruber, 1139 Afterglow Avenue, Great Pain, New Jersey." We didn't have ZIP codes in those days. Ergo: this bedsheet is not my bedsheet.'

Nevertheless, as no other bedsheet was to be found anywhere in the laundry room and all that Gail Schwartzendruber's search turned up was a closet with a toilet in it where a small dark man was fingering a hacksaw blade, and since Gail Schwartzendruber was on a strict budget and could not afford to lose a bedsheet at a point mid-way between the January white sales and the August white sales, she put the strange sheet into her blue plastic laundry basket and started up the stairs. She stopped under the fluorescent lights in the stairwell to examine once more the hem of the white side of the bedsheet. She could see now that the word 'REPENT' was not, as she had originally supposed, marked on the hem with a laundry pencil. It had been stitched into the fabric with glossy black thread. The fact that black thread had been chosen made it doubtful that the calligraphic embroidery was intended for a nuptial occasion.

PART II · *The Omen Fulfilled*

'Don't go too far from home,' said Mr and Mrs Schwartzendruber cautiously after Gail had finished college and was looking for a job. Caution was a habit they'd got into twenty years before when little Gail had begun to stray about the neighbourhood looking for someone to play with, and generally it's the repetition that makes a habit habitual. So Gail Schwartzendruber only went across the river to Manhattan. 'And only for a year or two,' she told her four new walls that were not new at all, but only new to her. 'Then I'm going to get married. Just as soon as Roger comes back from Bechuanaland.' She stood in the middle of the pitted linoleum floor and stretched out her arms. Tilting back her head, her eyes shut, she pivoted slowly and without taking a single step in any direction, brushed each wall in turn with her finger tips, vital components of her valuable manual dexterity.

PART III · *Bechuanaland*

Roger's two-year term with the Peace Corps in Bechuanaland had already been up for three years. When it had been up four years Gail Schwartzendruber was still working in Manhattan. Her new walls had aged amazingly over the interval. She had stopped brushing them with her finger tips and she rarely even spoke to them any more.

Roger's letters kept all their passion-riddled intensity but Roger himself did not come back from Bechuanaland. He lay stretched out in a hammock between a pair of baobab trees too moved by the thought of pale Gail Schwartzendruber to arise and go to the nearest airport. Sweet, pure, white Gail Schwartzendruber. He was not worthy to undo her topmost button.

He lifted a clipboard from its customary place on his lower right quadrant and began another letter.

It was all so different in Bechuanaland. Nothing buttoned.

PART IV · *The Letter*

'Even though I'm supposedly a healthy young man, no woman wants me. I used the computer last night to look at my problem. After calculating the present population of adult men and women over the age of 18 and below the age of 50 and then looking up some sizes of sexual organs in medical books, I discovered that there are approximately 24,600 kilometers of unused vagina in the United States every night and there aren't even six inches for me anywhere. It's hopeless.'

PART V · *Seldom Seen, Alabama*

Item from the society page of the *Seldom Seen Gazette*:

> In spite of a rough crossing (the North
> Atlantic is always rough at this time of
> year) Mrs Alice Organdorf, who is headed
> toward Europe on the 'Queen Mary', has
> been enjoying the trip. She has the distinc-
> tion of being the only American at the
> captain's table. Before boarding the ship in
> New York, daughter Sally Organdorf met
> her mother and the pair lunched, had
> dinner dates, and saw *La Plume de ma
> Tante* in that city. Since both Mrs Organ-
> dorf and Sally are avid workers for the Girl
> Scout movement, the two visited Scout
> headquarters in New York. On board ship
> Mrs Organdorf won first prize at a head-
> dress party when she appeared wearing a
> hair arrangement which depicted the song
> title 'La Vie en Rose'.

PART VI · *Weary*

Sally Organdorf was weary of Acapulco. After her mother
had sailed off into the North Atlantic with her hair
arrangement, speaking in American to the captain at his
table, Sally took a luxury apartment on the chic East Side.
Sally was weary also of her avid idleness. She took
employment at Scout headquarters. Finally, Sally was
weary of living in luxury all alone. She took Gail
Schwartzendruber, her former college room-mate, rent-
free for company.

Now Gail no longer had to wash her own bedsheets.
Every week Sally had the linen sent out, and the first time

Gail's went with it the strange bedsheet did not come back.

Sally covered the inside of the bathroom door with full-colour photographs of herself stretched out beside her Acapulco pool like a tigress on the chaise. 'Acapulco's a death trip,' Sally said to Gail.

PART VII · *She Considers Her Opportunities*

Because she now lived in luxury on the chic East Side Gail Schwartzendruber left the laboratory in the West Side hospital for the laboratory in another hospital much nearer, one to which she could walk, if necessary, in twenty minutes. The older single women in the new laboratory welcomed Gail warmly. They recognised one of their own, and Gail was twenty-seven years six months. But she did not agree. Sometimes she spoke of it to her centrifuge, in a low and secretive voice. 'I do not agree. I say "No, I am not like you. I am *not*." But they don't care what I say. They know what I am. I am one of them – one of the older single women on the laboratory staff. I am one of them and they are very friendly.'

She thought of Roger in Bechuanaland and knew their love was dead. She had been faithful for five years in Manhattan. Now she considered her opportunities. She was in the midst of a great city teeming with people at least half of whom, statistically speaking, were male. Even taking into account the fact that the huge majority of these males would be minors, married, senile, matachines, unsuitable colours or unscrupulous lechers, there still should remain, in a sample group so large, *someone* appropriate who was looking for a nice, twenty-seven-year-old girl to marry. A nice girl like Gail Marie Schwartzendruber. The thing was to find him before he heard of Bechuanaland.

PART VIII · *Beyond Bechuanaland*

In college Sally Organdorf had briefly been engaged to Jim
Flinchpaugh, who was famous on campus for being the
tallest, darkest, handsomest villain ever to come out of an
Arizona military academy. He had immediately left the
college and joined the air force when Sally, for generally
undisclosed reasons, broke off the engagement. 'He was
french-kissing me,' Sally confessed to Gail, 'and he
belched. That did it. I mean I know it was an accident, but
– God!' Although the relationship was definitely over Jim
and Sally made a friendly parting and they had continued
in a desultory way ever since to exchange joky cards.
Sally's featured ugly and impotent men. Jim's involved
innuendo and sexy girls. They rarely added anything, even
signatures, to the raunchy printed messages, but once
Sally wrote: *Remember Gail Schwartzendruber? Pale Gail
and Roger? Well, she's my room-mate again and a real
lonesome polecat. Roger's returned to the trees. I have it
on good authority that you're welcome.*

'Flinchpaugh's going to call you next time he's in town.
That is, if you're still interested.'

Gail was still interested. Perversely, someone else had
now become interested in Gail. He was an MD with just
a few months yet to intern and he seemed to spend most
of his time in the hospital in wrinkled green pyjamas
delivering babies. He really hadn't any business in the labs
but he justified himself: he was probably going to
specialize in gastro-enterology. Gail could always hear
him coming because he wore a brace. One of his legs
seemed to go all the way to the floor and the other to go
a bit further than that. Oddly, it was the leg that already
seemed too long that was so heavily braced.

Isadore ('Jock') Katz was beagle-faced, twenty-five, and
balding. Politely, during his third visit to Gail's laboratory
he asked if she would like to have a drink with him that

evening. After eight o'clock he'd be off duty until midnight. His first free evening in ten days. At midnight he'd begin another ten-day stretch on twenty-four-hour call. Gail was excited about having a date with a doctor. It was the ambition of every laboratory technician to date a doctor. If you could marry a doctor you were set up for life. Whooo-eeee!!! Gail's excitement affected her work. She spoiled three Sephadex columns that afternoon. 'Oh, aren't I scatterbrained!' she said to a beaker of gastric juice.

A few minutes before five o'clock Gail was summoned to the telephone. It was Lt James Flinchpaugh calling to say he had zeroed in on Floyd Mitchell Field just an hour before in his own jet fighter, that this time he'd remembered to lower his landing gear (because once he hadn't and it was very embarrassing) and would Gail like to go out with him to dinner that night. Gail said she already had a date for the evening, reminding Lt Flinchpaugh that he had never told her exactly when to expect him.

'So it's zilch, huh,' he said. 'Well, then. What about lunch tomorrow?'

'I think I can work that in.'

PART IX · Vertical/Horizontal

It was raining to quench hell when Jock Katz, MD, looking better in a suit than in green cotton pyjamas, called for Gail promptly at 8.30, apologizing for being late, complimenting her on her dress. 'I've only seen you in a lab coat before.'

'I've only seen *you* in green pyjamas.'

He held an umbrella over her, opened the car door for her, ('Watch that gutter – it's flooded'), closed the door after first making sure her feet were both inside. They drove to The Ginger Man and sat where they could see a Big TV Star feeding his date stingers. Jock's hand was always ready with the cigarettes, the lighter. He remembered the name of the town where Gail had gone to college and the name of the college and the name of the street in Great Pain, New Jersey, where her mother and father lived. Half an hour later, as they finished their second drink, Jock said, 'Shall we go?' He didn't say where they should go. It was only half past nine.

The poor medical student drove a late model Buick. He turned the key in the ignition but did not start the engine. Instead he took Gail Schwartzendruber's hands and put them over his crotch, at the same time forcing his mouth against hers, and he would have rammed his tongue down her throat if she hadn't reflexively clenched her jaws. With the stirrup of his brace he pushed a button on the dashboard and the backs of the car seats began to change from vertical to horizontal. Gail found herself looking at the upholstered ceiling. Her skirt seemed to be up around her ears and Jock's hands were tugging at the waistband of her tights. She sat up briskly, replacing her skirt and gripping her purse with both hands.

'What's wrong?' Jock had never met a girl before who didn't want a feel.

'It's rather complex,' said Gail staring through the rainy windshield. 'But basically his name is Roger and right now he's in Africa.'

Jock reclined on his elbow, his cheek in his palm, like a banqueting Caesar. 'How long since you saw him last?'

With all the dignity she had Gail Schwartzendruber answered. 'Five years.'

Jock pulled her towards him roughly, gripping her ankles between his feet (again his brace proved useful). Her hands were helpless in his and he placed them around his penis. His fly was open.

'Please. *Quit* it.'

'I'm sorry, baby. I don't get turned on so often, you know. Working a schedule like mine.' Jock spoke softly, without the least embarrassment, as he pulled on the tab of her back-zippered dress.

'Then *quit* it,' said Gail, tugging herself free.

'I said I was sorry.'

'*Okay* then.' Gail moved over into her own seat and sat there stiffly. 'Couldn't you please put the backs up again?'

'Okay then,' echoed Jock politely, pushing Gail down on her back and sprawling over her as though she had given him, not forgiveness, but permission to continue. As though if he said often enough that he was sorry it would be quite all right to go on with the rape. Weighting her body with his he whispered: 'I find you very touching, baby. Do you know you make me go around the wards humming "Moon River"?'

'I find *you* very touching too,' said Gail in a cold fury. 'Now back off and sail away.'

'Look,' Jock said. 'If you haven't had a man in *five years* . . . '

'Take me home, please.'

'Look. Relax. Enjoy it. It doesn't have to mean a thing. Come on, baby. Take me.'

'*You* take *me* home. Now.' Anger gave Gail the strength she needed to throw Jock off and to sit up, this time feeling for the handle to her door. 'I don't have to give my body to anyone who buys me two drinks and keeps me dry in the rain.'

'I was nice to you, wasn't I. Now why the hell can't you reciprocate.'

'Are you going to take me home?'

'*Okay*, if that's the way you feel.'

'That's the way I feel.'

They drove back in silence. At Gail's apartment she didn't wait for Dr Katz to come round to open her door or hold an umbrella over her head or remind her about the gutter. She stumbled out of the car and through the foyer, past the doorman and into the elevator without a glance behind her. Jock, who had no reason any more to open doors or umbrellas for Gail Marie Schwartzendruber, had hardly waited for his car door to close again before he drove off.

Sally was out – she liked to mooch around Harlem at night – and the apartment was dark. The sound of steam hissing in the radiators inflated the silent rooms to bursting. Gail stood under the shower, finishing off a bottle of Sally's Chivas Regal, alternately rinsing out her mouth and drinking deep swallows, each swallow causing her to choke and shudder. 'Anything goes,' she said to the bottle. 'It's form that counts. Rape with murmured apologies. He'd have bought you like a whore for a couple of drinks . . . for a couple of lousy drinks. Dr Veneer . . . Dr Venereal . . . Not me. I'm not for sale. Or for rent. Or for ninety-nine year lease . . . I'm free, Doctor. I'm not loose. I am *free*. Can you perceive, Doctor, that there is a difference?'

PART X · Fiduciary Matters

Gail woke with an aching head. Far, far away at the other end of herself loomed her feet. They were cold and slippery with sweat. Slowly she moved one hand over the surface of her night-table trying to locate the alarm clock without having either to turn her head or to focus her eyes. Nudged over the table-edge by Gail's dextrous fingers a pair of glasses clattered to the floor. 'Hell's *bells*!' She found the clock and held it up to her eyes. It was, good God, only 6.35. Why was she awake so early? Why was she lying so stiff and so straight upon her back, like an arranged corpse? Very carefully she lifted herself on to her elbow and looked over at Sally's slumbering hulk. *She* was beached in dreamland, all right. Sally could always sleep until nearly nine o'clock any weekday morning because she was an Organdorf. Unlike Gail, she never attempted to cope with breakfast or with any of the finer points of personal good grooming. Sally Organdorf, fat and rich and relaxed, could afford all her carelessness.

Gail lay back and listened to her pulse, which was like the surf roaring in a seashell. She must take some aspirin. Unsteadily, she got up and immediately all her body's blood plunged to her feet. There was an electric buzzing inside both her legs. Under the skin her veins writhed and tangled. She drew a glass of warm water from the bathroom tap, tossed two aspirin down her throat and poured the water after them. Back in her cold bed she slipped into a strangely populated sleep. The phone ringing in the room brought her plummeting out of her weightless dream-float. It seemed she was being hurtled at her bed; that she struck it with the whole prone length of her body. She shuddered and lay still. A classic clonic jerk. Sally had picked up the phone. It was Mrs Canfield, Sally's supervisor at Scout headquarters. Mrs Canfield was apt to telephone on mornings when she especially wanted Sally to be at work on time. Sally was, by her own account, 'not a morning person' and Mrs Canfield was resigned to this except in times of emergency. With the International Triennial Conference in Detroit only a month away it was a time of emergency.

'Jesus, it's only 7.30,' Sally grumped, hanging up the phone and falling back upon her bed. It gasped at the blow, then the room was silent. Before Gail could turn over Sally was asleep again.

When Gail awoke for the third time that morning she saw Sally sitting in her slip on the edge of her bed, a shoe dangling heelwise from her index finger. She was staring at the floor. From the ashtray beside her foot a cigarette launched its thin blue ribbon into the still air. It was nine twenty-five. Sally called Mrs Canfield and told her she would be at the office in ten minutes. Half an hour later she put on her dress and left.

By taking a cab Gail reached the lab shortly before eleven. Lt Flinchpaugh arrived smartly at twelve, dressed in a blue uniform and so handsome he was literally beautiful. 'Miss Gail Schwartzendruber, I presume,' he said as he came into her laboratory. His smile nearly put out her aching eyes. She had forgotten all about him. 'Well – hello dere.' He had the kind of bass voice that shakes glass; her lab was all a-tremble.

'Hello,' said Gail.

'You are looking lovely, Miss Schwartzendruber. Prettier than ever.'

Gail looked at his tanned, perfect skin, remembered the pimple forming on her chin, thanked him and excused herself. 'Just let me get out of this lab coat and I'll be right with you.'

In the washroom she examined her skin to see if it was as bad as she thought it was. The mirror and the fluorescent light brought in an immediate, unanimous verdict: it was worse. A young technician from the laboratory next to Gail's followed her into the washroom. '*Who* is that *dreamy* guy?'

'Oh, just someone I knew in school.'

'You goin' out with 'im?'

'Just for lunch.'

'Boy, am I green!' The girl smirked and puckered her mouth. 'Well – have fun!'

'Okay,' said Gail. 'I'll try.'

The only other person in the elevator with them was Monty, its operator, but Jim Flinchpaugh pressed himself up tight against Gail as though the car were jammed. In mock apology he said, 'I'm sorry it's so crowded in this elevator, ma'm.' Gail pretended to give him a punch in the midriff. 'It isn't *that* crowded, Lieutenant.' Monty turned around with a big smile just in time to see Gail get a kiss on the cheek.

'You know,' said Lt Flinchpaugh, 'I thought for sure

you'd be married by now and have seven or eight kids.'

They had lunch at The Showplace, a happy change from the hospital cafeteria. Flinchpaugh didn't drink and so Gail went without the Bloody Mary she now realized she'd just about been living for. Certainly she wasn't hungry. The lieutenant thought it nice Gail didn't drink. 'I really like that in a girl.' Gail thought of the preceding evening and felt iniquitous. According to college rumour Jim Flinchpaugh had a brother who was an alcoholic. Jim didn't mention his brother but he said he'd seen what liquor did to people and he was glad Gail didn't use it.

Use it, she thought. As though it were Listerine.

Jim Flinchpaugh told her he had now definitely decided to give up his air force career. He wanted to come to New York and be a musical comedy star. A big talent agency had already approached him about it.

After lunch Lt Flinchpaugh reluctantly returned Gail to her work. He had to fly back to Miami that afternoon, and before he did he wanted to kiss her. A proper kiss. In his opinion, which he solemnly reported to her, she had a classic beauty. But this time the elevator was loaded with technicians, three crates of hamsters, and a couple of bales of hay for the Animal Room.

In the hall outside Gail's laboratory Lt Flinchpaugh at least got both his arms round her. People in white coats kept passing them. The same people, Gail was sure. Going back and forth and back and forth. There had never been such traffic in the corridor before. Gail felt intensely foolish standing pinioned to the wall by Lt Flinchpaugh's embrace, pinioned and exposed to the whole hospital staff. Everyone was going to get the wrong idea. Lt Flinchpaugh stared at her. Finally he wrinkled his forehead and spoke. 'Well now, you sure are a pretty one.' And that said, he kissed her on the mouth.

'I ought to get a drink of water before I go back to work.

There's a fountain down by the elevator.' Lt Flinchpaugh stepped aside then, taking her hand and holding it up in a courtly way, as though he were about to ask her to waltz. Oh yes, thought Gail Schwartzendruber. Let's *do*! She'd never waltzed in her life. It would be lovely to waltz. She'd always thought so. *There* might be a pattern to reform the design of her life. But Lt Flinchpaugh was soberly studying the palm of Gail's hand for signs of luck and destiny. He insisted he could see remarkable things in Gail's future. 'Look at this.' He held out his other hand, palm up. 'This line right here. Now then. Compare it with yours right *there*. See? As near as identical where this line and that line in your palm meet and where they meet in mine. I call that very significant. And notice the way these joined-up lines go off into five little ones over the edge of the palm there. You know what those are?' His finger passed delicately through the crotch formed by Gail's thumb and first finger. 'Children.' The sensation produced by his finger moving lightly over the palm of her hand made Gail want to feel it move over her whole body, which she would give as bare to him as her palm. Her hand would imitate his until they both felt that slow, cumulative tickle, artfully prolonged and resisted. Such touching as became a pollen on their flesh to make it itch and weep.

Gail laughed and spun away from him, pivoting in the deserted area-way beside the elevator and the drinking fountain. She bent to drink. Lt Flinchpaugh's glossy boot pressed the pedal. Sweet soft water flowed into Gail's mouth. 'That's sure *one* thing about New York,' he said. 'Good water. The stuff we get at the base comes fresh from the Everglades. Of course, it's all a plot to sell more orange juice.'

'Damn it. Oh damn it,' thought Gail. 'He really does like me.' It unnerved her. It panicked her into lying. 'I ought to have told you,' she said. 'I had a wire this morning from

Roger. He's coming back from Bechuanaland next week. We're going to get married.'

PART XI · *Next week in Acapulco*

'I'm going back to Acapulco next week,' said Sally Organdorf to Gail Schwartzendruber. 'Working's a drag.'

PART XII · *Oolong Tea*

Now, even though Gail had moved back to the West Side, the older single women in her laboratory closed ranks around her. She was invited to their apartments for dinner. She was asked to join them as a group at Radio City Music Hall on Saturday afternoons where they stood in line with the tourists to see 'My Fair Lady' or 'The Sound of Music'. Once, as by accident, they saw 'Juliet of the Spirits' instead of 'Mary Poppins' and they came away silenced, disturbed by all that ripeness. Walking to Schrafft's afterwards they asked one another vaguely, 'Well, what did *you* make of it?' At Schrafft's they ate chicken *à la king* and drank Oolong tea and talked about the doctors and liver perfusion and paper electrophoresis and through all their talking each one could hear the answer standing attentively behind her, like a treacherous serving-maid.

PART XIII · *A Good People*

Winds from everywhere parachute into town. They take over the streets. Upset steel cages. Litter runs free. Papers race down the avenues, buckling walkers' knees, lodging between their feet. The invaders consolidate. Winds become one wind. A direction agreed upon, the air rushes to the sea. It draws frowns on every face. Shakes shop windows. The solidest reflection shivers. Thin ginkgos rattle in their palings. The wind parts the long hair of girls and throws it into their eyes. It pulls up skirts and steals hats. It rips the flags of all nations. It shreds shop awnings. It empties lungs. The domestic emblems that hang protected in tall nooks among the tenement walls whip and crackle on their lines, but they are not hauled in. With every sheet and shirt and towel the ordinary women of Manhattan, the wives and mothers of the poor, signal to one another: we are at home; we have hung out the week's wash; all is well with us.

In the West 70s an oedematous old woman sits all day on a fish box by the door of a condemned tenement. She wears a rubber khaki raincoat and a railway engineer's striped cap. Like the windows above her head each of her eyes is taped with a white X. She heaps the street like a pile of God's shit.

In fumes of intense light the park smoulders. For seven weeks there has been no rain. All ornamental fountains in the city have been shut off. The people are requested to limit the frequency of their baths and the duration of their showers. Water is not served in restaurants unless specifically ordered. The streets are damped once each week with undrinkable water from the Hudson, as it shrinks from its own stinking banks of mud. Swimming pools everywhere are closed, but the beaches remain open to the public, for the sea water already contains the filth, heat and saltiness of the public's own sweat and excrement. The mayor has asked his citizens to attend with tap water any municipal trees planted near their buildings, first spading the hard inches of earth the trees live in, to let the water through. Most of the people, having no earth of their own, have no buckets or spades. Housewives hack at the ground with tablespoons. They dole out water in Pyrex cups to the plane trees and the ginkgos.

In the cindered park grey squirrels sit in drinking fountains whose basins are as dry as the earth. A young man walking through the park turns the handles on the fountains. At his approach the squirrels leap out and crouch not far off. They curve bald tails over their backs and watch him. Disease has spoiled their coats. The young man closes the mouth of each fountain drain with leaves dropped from trees that should still be green. He turns the chromium knob. A delicate sheath of water films the fountain-head. When he has gone away water is in the fountain; grey squirrels are drinking. In the night rain falls. By morning the park's asphalt paths glitter with puddles of fresh water.

In the East 70s Mrs Alice Organdorf, happily widowed, ageing into blonde, smiles tenderly at her chihuahua peeing on a ginkgo.

How gentle we are to our animals! Surely, we are a good people.

Threadball

The very stones of the buildings he passed walking east across midtown began to seem unstable, dangerously soft, puffy. They looked as if they were liquifying internally, dissolving in secret rottenness. He had to reach out and press his fingertips against the limestone facing of the Chemical Bank of New York so that the gritty tingle of the grain in it on his flesh could reassure him of its unassailable solidity. I must be going mad, he thought.

A scrap of white paper fluttered in the void over his head. Mostly it rocked to and fro in the moil of the rainy wind, but it was also steadily losing altitude as it went before him, as if it wanted him for something. He started to imagine it was a note from Susannah and that she had tossed it out of the window of the transcontinental bus she'd just left town on. As soon as the paper came within his reach he would pluck it from the wind and find that it said Darling, changed my mind – meet me at the Port Authority in 20 minutes.

It could never be. Susannah was the most resolute woman on earth.

An empty sandwich bag skated ahead of him on the sidewalk, gliding north, planing south, reeling, stumbling, lifting. Has a life of its own, he thought. Susannah would have said it had no more life of its own than the people here have. Well, Susannah was out of it all. She was gone. She'd given up. But he was still hanging in, even if it was only by his thumbs. When he came out on to Fifth Avenue the air was thready with rain. The great avenue gleamed like a river. Small ripples steadily crossed it from kerb to kerb, helped on by the wheels. Midtown teemed with people. His imagination turned them all to water. The gutters swirled with opaque water, all that remained of a million people. It certainly reminded him of spilled chocolate malteds but for once did not induce him to look for the nearest soda fountain. He headed uptown through all the grey, slippery beauties of the day. The peacock spots of motor oil on asphalt still seemed as satisfying to him as they had been the day his infant eye first registered them spread like silk antimacassars on his grandfather's drive in Scarsdale. His first aesthetic experience.

He especially loved New York in thick weather; loved the exact, receding ranges of the East Side, ghostly cluster of towers beyond the Park. Susannah had wanted to turn him against the city the way she had turned against it and she tried to enforce on him her preference for 'the velvet on the hill' – her way of referring to that blue plush effect on mountains whose very existence depended upon your never getting within twenty miles of it. Her 'velvet' was a metaphor for keeping your distance. Maybe she'd hoped he hadn't noticed that. As for her nonsense about 'no nature in the city' and therefore no sense of changing seasons, as far as he was concerned there was never a more perfect image for spring than the luminosity of a young ailanthus in new leaf against the dark, experienced stones of Trinity Church. For him even the swift billowing of smoke-shadows across the blank end-wall of International Flavours and Fragrances was a manifestation of nature's flux. In the first scant brightness of the day those shadows from the Con Edison chimneys were like the flickerings of big wings, and as the sun started from the roof and slowly pressed the darkness down that wall all the way to the street the shadows rippled on an ever-enlarging field of turkey-red brick. 'That's nature in abundance!' he had said to Susannah, pointing out the wall early one morning. 'That's pollution,' Susannah had said back smartly.

How they had argued it!

Replaying their old, somehow delightful disagreements he nearly passed on by Gristede's boy squatting in the gutter among brilliant liquids and plastic-wrapped wreckage from his over-turned delivery bike.

'Hey, buddy, you OK?'

'I *look* OK? Mothuhfuckuh.'

As he approached his own building he automatically fell into step with the brisk plonk CRASH plonk CRASH plonk CRASH of a pile-driver at work nearby. It's a demolition zoo, this town, Susannah had said. We're all exhibits in a zoo. He had pretended to search his navel for lint when she said that, and to tickle his armpits and comb his fingers through the hair on his chest. To satisfy him she'd laughed, and he'd dropped the monkey bit and said, 'Anyway, if we've got to be behind bars it might as well be the bar at the Bottom Line. Find out how they've managed so long without us. Put on your clothes.'

Happy days.

Across the street was a giraffe's pasture – what Susannah called the construction site at the end of his block, because a forty-storey crane stood in there behind a fence made of doors. Even that – a lot of old tenement doors tacked together – was New York to him. Pure show biz. You could make a great stage set out of old doors like that. All colours, scuffed, graffitied. Doors people had once found a minute's peace and privacy behind, in the bathroom, in the bedroom – licit, illicit. It was the perfect set for a farce. 'And we're the perfect farce for the set,' said Susannah, stepping with theatrical gestures into the spotlight of his memory.

Up in the duplex he stood at the parapet of his terrace and looked down at the ant-like activities in the street. Susannah always told him it was corrupting to live where you could look down on so many of your fellows. 'I belong down there,' she'd told him, 'and when I'm down there it's crazy to look up and see trees growing three hundred, four hundred feet from the ground.' And all the windows – 'One million sore eyes' Susannah said. He'd called to her once: 'Come out here and see the African villages,' meaning the coolie-hatted water tanks up on stilts among the slant skylights and elevator penthouses on the roofs of the older buildings. 'Yeah,' she said. Sometimes he doubted whether she had any imagination at all.

Now if he wanted to he could spend the rest of the day looking down, or watching the forty-storey crane move its slow, browsing, prehistoric head stiffly back and forth. 'Inertia's your problem, boy,' he told himself, settling into his Eames chair. 'Lie on your butt and dream. You whose idea of strenuous activity is getting out of bed for lunch.' He would let his memory just fill and float him to the top of the cistern of life. Happy days. And the happiest of all – the day Susannah had told him that while riding downtown to work on the IRT she had decided that the two of them were compatible. He hadn't analyzed her choice of words at the time. It had been no time for analysis. What she was saying and what he perfectly understood was that she loved him. And the only thing to do about that was what they'd done: grinned goofy grins at each other over the table for the rest of the meal. It was later that he noticed the actual words she'd chosen on that famous night. He'd decided to write them down, suddenly anxious that something he had been effortlessly remembering every two or three minutes for a month was abruptly going to slip out of his mind and elude him forever. 'I've decided we're compatible.' Those were her exact words. He even discovered when he thought about it that he possessed a mnemonic device for making sure of the crucial word. He knew she'd said 'compatible' because it had reminded him of his father's joke about incompatibility as grounds for divorce. Punch line: the husband had no income and the wife wasn't pat-able.

That of course reminded him of *his* wife. It started him wandering through the duplex, beset by an intolerable restlessness. As from noon today he had neither mistress nor wife beside him. In the living room, which he'd hardly entered since the unpat-able Gretchen left him, there were still some of her magazines lying about. He picked one up, feeling more as though he were in a dentist's waiting room than in any place of his own. The magazine fell open at the horoscope feature. Over a box outlined in stars were the words BIRTHDAY GREETINGS, HEAVENLY TWINS. Inside the box was 'May 21 - June 22: Gemini. Day mansion of Mercury, sanguine, changeable, and commanding; and airy, hot and moist in nature. Principle house of Saturn, masculine diurnal signs, fixed and sanguine . . . ' What *is* this crap? 'With you Geminis it's mind over heart. You are intellectuals who operate with your brains, not your emotions. Your dual personalities make you quick to get angry, quick to cool down. Very happy, very sad. Geminis have inquiring and perceptive minds; you learn and remember easily. Your inquisitiveness occasionally causes you to spread too thin, becoming fascinated with one project after another.' They can get right down to it sometimes, he thought, but this astrology stuff is garbage. 'Geminis are good at languages and facts and figures.' Especially figures. He leered and waggled his eyebrows at the opposite chair as though Susannah sat there. 'You are romantic but flighty and flirtatious.' NOT flirtatious – that's calumny! 'You can settle down eventually but you need a mate (Aries, Libra, Leo or Aquarius are best) . . . '

Gretchen, of course, was also a Gemini 'but your attitude of mind over emotion can make you seem unsympathetic and cold.' True, too true, alas, alas. 'You have a tendency to be self-centred and flip.' Really! 'Under extreme pressure you can also be untruthful.' That's a lie! 'Your colours are orange and violet (sometimes blue).' Oh yes, often blue . . . 'Wednesday is your day.'

He sat down and considered this compendium of attributes and fortunes. As it was now Thursday yesterday had been 'his day'. All he could say was that it had not *seemed* to be, judging by what had happened on it. Perhaps, everything considered, the part he'd liked best was that 'Day mansion of Mercury' stuff. It was like poetry. You couldn't pin it down. The rest of it, though, was just flattery and guesswork. Cunning, though, to take the sting out of every little defect by providing a reason for it. If a Gemini is ever untruthful it is only 'under extreme pressure'. Susannah had told him that he suffered from velleity. Velleity of the second definition, that is. Incomplete volition. He certainly wasn't troubled with velleity of the primary definition: the lowest degree of desire. How would an astrologer soften the curse of incomplete volition, he wondered. 'But only when there's nothing to choose between?' In the end he went back to the part about 'sanguine, changeable, commanding'. He liked that. He felt like that. Those were qualities he could illustrate. He saw himself illustrating them. He saw himself standing with military bearing upon a pedestal in Grand Army Plaza (for he had been born in Brooklyn Heights). He wore his shower kilt. His legs were among his best features.

He tried another magazine. Some of the lingerie ads were quite provoking examples of soft porn. Women wouldn't look at them that way, he assumed. At least not most women. Isn't that what they say? He realized next that he didn't know who he meant by 'they'. Experts, he supposed. People trained to look into our attitudes and design questionnaires and ask ordinary women about things. There *are* ordinary women. His mother had been one. So had Gretchen. Well – hadn't she? She *appeared* to be ordinary. But *was* she? Going on and on and on that time about the Lindseys' adopted baby. How darling he was, how cute, how sweet, how adorable. And not going on to the Lindseys themselves so much as pointing her remarks at *him*. Later, back home, more and more about the Lindseys' baby. What was it all about? He never knew. If Gretchen wanted a baby why didn't she say so? She would never – this is incredible, he thought – allow him to take the necessary – steps. Gretchen, his wife of five years, was a virgin to this day. They had never even discussed children. Just for some reason she'd taken in a big way to that adopted kid. It didn't signify. Oh yes it did. Yes, it did. He could hear her voice full of wistfulness. Yes, indeed. He hadn't picked up on it at the time. Or he had pushed it away. Yes. He'd heard it and pushed it away. What else could he do? Gretchen baffled him. She considered sex to be an attack upon her person with a blunt instrument. Okay. A cock *is* a blunt instrument, if you like. And would you prefer to imagine a sharp one? He ought to have asked her.

His eye was caught by a photograph of – of what? An ear, apparently, surrounded by fuzz. No. Couldn't be. Two little central holes in it, a perfectly bevelled rim. No clue at all except the name of a Fifth Avenue women's tailor. So, why this ear? Why wasn't Gretchen here to explain . . . no! This was not a puzzle fit for a male Gemini's mind. 'I blush for myself,' he said aloud, testing his voice on the emptiness of the room. 'It's a nasal voice, isn't it. Oh Susannah, don't you blush for me . . . '

He returned to his study. It was approaching rush hour, to judge by the decibel count which was high now even on this high floor. Susannah was probably being borne down the Pennsylvania Turnpike, through Penn's spindly woods. The rain made it seem darker and later than it was. Now it was time to play that prayer out of Mozart's

'Requiem' for the deliverance of the souls of the faithful departed. Especially he looked forward to that part when all the voices that have ever uttered on earth seem to surge jubilantly towards God, irresistibly shouting You *promised* us, You *promised* us, You *promised* us. He would cause this to sound over the heads of the heedless multitude down there who were filling up the trains and buses and cabs and sidewalks, hurrying home to Scarsdale, or to some delicious assignation elsewhere. *Quam olim Abrahae promisisti et semini ejus.* It excited him to conjoin those two crowds: the members of Paradise and the exhibits in the demolition zoo. He turned the volume as high as it would go, four hundred watts to each speaker, and opened the terrace windows. Let the rain blow in. To hell with it.

The record finished and clicked off. He lay on his back and dreamed a dream in which everyone now in the world put off his inhibitions and prohibitions and simply grabbed the nearest person and fell to joyfully. Nothing was forbidden. All partners were good, none was preferred over another. No one held back, demurred or refused. He could see Gretchen happily screwing. Ecstatically happy. He'd never seen her look like that. Never supposed she *could* look like that. He remembered she used to laugh a bit that way when he was clowning around, doing his Bob & Ray bits in the campus coffee bar. Gretchen had had flush and sparkle at those moments, giggling away at his antics. And that was how he thought she was all the time. He realized it now. In his mind he pictured her as she'd been, the heaviness of her nose and jaw subdued to the whiteness of her teeth, her head tilted back with laughter, the long flat planes of her cheeks broken up by that transverse happy mouth. And yet she really wasn't like that at all.

What a good dream it had been! He'd write it down in a minute for Susannah. How all the sad people had turned to happy people and no one pined for another and no one renounced anything and no one was afraid of anything. No one had whipped or threatened or degraded or refused anyone else and there was someone desirable for everyone. The whole world had been happy for once. And he was happy too. 'Hey, Gretchen! Susannah! When do we leave for happiness?'

Nothing answered him, of course.

It was dinner-time now and there was no food ready. Gretchen had always had an excellent meal for him when he came in. She had never let him down on that score. He wandered into the kitchen with its empty wine rack, its red and white checkered country curtains with the ball fringe that was sooty now, the remains of his breakfast on the table. 'Shit,' he said. He pushed up the lid on the bread bin. A slow fly wandered out and crept off into the air, leaving the bin empty. 'Shit.' The refrigerator contained quantities of ice and something furry in a bowl. Finally he came across half a packet of saltines at the back of a cupboard. He chewed one while the fly crawled through the stagnant air, round and round above the squalid table. The fly irritated him for its lack of initiative. It would neither leave the kitchen nor alter its air-speed. It maundered along past his nose tracking the edge of the table until eventually it passed his nose again. Without the slightest exertion he could have closed his fist around it. He couldn't be bothered. It wasn't because he was a merciful man. He just couldn't be bothered to kill a fly.

The
Mama
Stories

' . . . there is no salvation in becoming adapted
to a world which is crazy.' – *Henry Miller*

Bridger's Moth
Wool
The Persistence of Rathbun

Bridger's Moth

By the time she was sixteen Mama had finished with her crushes on female school teachers. After that her fantasy was to inspire some masterly 'older man' of famous good character and worldly achievement with the grandest passion of his life. For when Mama fell in love she should not be as her chums already were – pining after boys like puppies who lived under jalopies and only came out to eat supper. Mama would fall in love like the nymphs of antiquity: with a river that she could follow to the sea.

This fantasy sustained Mama through her crucial under-graduate years. Then, all of a sudden, it was translated, however inadequately, into the realities of flesh. Mama's 'masterly older man' was no less a figure than the President of The Christian Institution, which meant that within his sphere he was all things to all men. Now a man who is all things to all men is of no use whatsoever to a woman. Most women know this. They have a strong practical instinct about it and do not waste their time. Mama had no such instinct. She had to be instructed. The man who instructed her, by his example, was President Bridger.

Bridger was not the answer to a maiden's prayer, for he never answered prayers from maidens, but to any hostess he was the obligingly ideal 'extra man' and brides adored him. All through the year he had invitations to hundreds of parties and, particularly in June, to scores of weddings. Whenever he could he attended the important ones but to every bride, whether he would witness her nuptials or not, he sent a gift of Steuben glass. Thus there never was an evening when Bridger had nothing in particular to do. He was never far from a packed bag. A man in his position had ever to be attuned to the whims of the rich, poised to seize the moment when their thoughts should turn, great with golden resolution, to the eleemosynary. Wherever they might be he must be ready to go himself, at any time, to accept their beneficence, and, when it was absolutely unavoidable, their advice on higher education. Some of Bridger's busier weeks passed with no acknowlegement of the sleeping hours at all but one dawn melted into the next as he changed trains in Chicago or waited in a cold wooden station for a connection at the Orrville Junction, or studied a dossier in a roomette on the Pennsylvania Railroad to prepare for breakfast in Wall Street with a semi-repentant stock market confidence man. If the names he could not help dropping now and then struck the ear with the chime of solid gold, it was not Bridger's fault.

Bridger had been President of The Christian Institution for seventeen years – a record-setting tenure in that line of work. He was admirably candid about his success and the luxurious fringe of benefits that went with it. 'Frankly, I like luxury,' he would say, usually to one young lady or another, 'but I have never had the slightest desire to own anything.' Thus, in The Motor Age, Bridger did not possess a motor car. His Lincoln and its driver were supplied by

The Christian Institution, which also provided his Georgian colonial residence and the antiques in it, the nine-foot Steinway he liked to play after dinner for his guests, and his perfectly plain and plain-spoken housekeeper, Maud. Though neither life nor The Christian Institution had equipped Bridger with a wife he did not feel any lack. For his hostess on official occasions he had his mother. He did not require a wife. Bridger's sole personal indulgence was not books (people gave him books all the time – more than even *he* could read). Bridger's sole personal indulgence was the society of pretty young women possessing the usual range of cultivated interests to be expected in girls with Higher Educations and Serious Attitudes. Of course Bridger was surrounded by such creatures at The Christian Institution – surrounded to his delight – but being so often away from the small town The Institution crowned gave him scope to extend his interests. One might say he collected young ladies from a wide range of habitats. He was always scouting for specimens.

Sex, of course, was out of the question for the President of The Christian Institution, yet even for a man in his position Bridger's continence would have been legendary were it not for the fact that so many women could testify to its actuality on the most literal level. It had never dismayed Bridger – it had pleasantly surprised him – how many charming girls (indeed, how many charming *matrons*) had at one time or another rolled over, so to speak, and offered their aid to the relief of his virginity. Bridger never had any difficulty in keeping a grip on himself when presented with these delightfully threatening postures. Bridger could be surprised, but he could not be taken by surprise. He would thank the woman sincerely for the offer of her self and earnestly assure her that, however regrettable it might be, copulation was out of the question. 'Don't misunderstand me,' he'd say. 'I'm very much flattered that you should want to but as a bachelor and a committed Christian I'm simply barred from this sort of thing.' It was part of Bridger's charm and tact that he always managed this phase of a relationship so as not to allow it to reflect upon the woman's own presumed commitment to *her* virginity – or her spouse. Bridger was as renowned for tact and charm as for being handsome, tall and dark, thus ever after providing Mama with a full description of a typical villain.

Bridger's goal for everyone was excellence in everything. He himself had long been a model of this goal. At Yale in the 30s he'd been the most cunning quarterback in the Ivy League – the wittiest of companions at dinner – the cleverest of partners at bridge, the most thorough scholar, the poet of amateur pianists and, after the age of nineteen, the sole support of his widowed mother. He was modest, unsparing of himself, hard-working, cheerful, yet, in material terms at least, curiously unambitious. Such a man is a born steward. To him parents entrust their children, husbands their wives, wives their lovers, rich men their money, philosophers their thoughts, sinners their confessions. In the seventeen years of Bridger's leadership of The Christian Institution where he himself had been an undergraduate, he had raised both the endowment and the moral tone above anything they'd ever achieved before him. Everyone admired him. Not a few venerated him. Even the small 'liberal element' on the faculty, to whom Bridger represented everything it most wanted to get rid of, did not really want to get rid of Bridger. At the age of fifty-two he was as secure and respected as a bishop. No. More respected than that. His spirit and his flesh were pure.

Bridger did not smoke or drink and was not delighted by women who did. Albeit, when he was first getting to know a young lady he always offered cigarettes and suggested wine with dinner. The wise and the careful would gracefully refuse. The others would accept what appealed to them, only to find that ever afterwards Bridger was too occupied to see them again, only giving them a telephone call once a year from the other side of the country. Bridger had a rationale, and knowing that every woman was going to require a rationale sooner or later he presented his very openly at an early stage in the relationship. If two friends are true friends, went Bridger's rationale, their relationship will survive all silence, all distance, all time elapsed, and can be resumed with no awkwardness at any time circumstances combine to bring the friends together again, and so on and so forth. Bridger's rationale was the solace of more than one neglected young lady who had once been foolish enough to accept a cigarette before dinner.

When The Christian Institution had invited Bridger to its presidency he accepted with the conviction that although he himself was only a humble scholar he knew deep in his heart that he had a vocation to lead The Institution through the years ahead. It was God's will. Events proved that the team of God & Bridger Inc. was a terrific success. Together they talked millions out of steel and soap and rubber and oil and Wall Street and Washington. 'Actually, you know, I'm a pretty shy bird,' Bridger liked to say, especially to a young lady, 'but when you care as much about something as I care about The Christian Institution there's just nothing you wouldn't do to help it prosper.'

Bridger handled his nation-wide network of young ladies as successfully as he managed the affairs of the Institution, speaking to each girl of his sense of personal responsibility for her, showing her the same degree of personal concern he had for a millionaire's widow or a promising Freshman fullback. The outcome of Bridger's skilful management was nearly always as pleasing to Bridger as it was to the young ladies, for each would eventually marry some suitable doctor or lawyer or member of the Junior Chamber of Commerce. Bridger would remain in touch with each couple, who would invite him to dinner whenever he was in the area. He could watch them becoming families – one boy, one girl, one household pet (which Bridger always hoped would not be a cat, for cats gave him horripilation). After a pleasant evening he could return to his hotel room at a reasonable hour satisfied that all was right with the nation. Life was proceeding just as it should in seemliness and prosperity. All his young friends were doing well and in time could be expected to do well by The Christian Institution's endowment fund. Nor would they neglect to.

'Bridger is absolutely *married* to The Christian Institution.' Bridger knew that people said this about him all the time and he was not displeased. As he had told Mama and most of the other young ladies he liked, 'If a man can channel his sexual energies into something higher, why, I think that's wonderful.' It often seemed to Bridger that a lot of other people were always trying to sublimate everything else into *sex*. Bridger only thought about sex when, as President of The Christian Institution, it was his clear duty to. The Institution's policy on pre-marital, extra-marital and unconventional sex was well understood by the students and faculty alike, in consequence of which they usually refrained from copulating on Institution property, even if the partners were legally entitled to enjoy one another. Nevertheless, from time to time some private coupling or other would become the concern of the Institution and then Bridger would have to meet with the deans, who were all married persons, and study what to do about the indecorum. One day when Bridger convened a meeting to consider a particularly troublesome case of this kind he remarked by way of starting things off that he had never before had to think so deeply about a subject from which he could expect to obtain so little personal pleasure. This comment was added to the 'Bridger stories', of which there was by that time a great lore, crowned by his saying when told that the Board of Trustees had decided to name the new student union building after him:

'Isn't that the height of wishful thinking – to name a union after a bachelor!'

Bridger's mother was a mischievous old lady, who winked her gentian eye at every young woman Bridger asked her to invite for a weekend, promising that Bridger intended to marry her. 'He talks about you all the time,' she'd say to the wretched girl, who, never having heard a word of marriage or anything like it from son Bridger would nevertheless begin inwardly to triumph. Bridger's mother rejoiced at no sight more than that of a pretty young thing with the wind in her sails and the reef at her keel.

When Mama received her invitation from Mrs Bridger to spend a weekend at the President's residence she studied the shivering, infirm hand in which it was written and allowed herself a moment's jubilation. '*She's* not going to last forever – just look at that handwriting!' Mama had heard that it was only on account of his mother that Bridger had never married, but Mama ignored the implications of this. Mama could tell from the things Bridger had said to her and written to her in his occasional letters that ever since she had entered his life he had felt profoundly shaken. Mama was very slow to catch on, people said afterwards.

Mama had never counted it anything but an advantage that Bridger was so much older than she. Mama held that once a human mind was matured the physical age of the body is irrelevant. Between childhood and senility life moves through a fertile plateau. Tilth for the spirit and the intellect. Common ground. But while Mama gladly acceded to a sort of universal physical democracy she recognized that an aristocracy of the mind plainly existed and she cared, in truth, only for its members. Bridger was the first man she'd ever met of whom she could entirely approve. There had been one or two boys while Mama was growing up who had considered her attractive enough to grope in school assembly movies but nothing on earth could induce Mama to spend any of her after-school time with them. She had laid upon one and all the curse of 'lackwit'. 'You've got to give them a chance,' her mother had pleaded. 'Don't judge them by what they are now. Try to see their potential. What will they be like in ten years?' 'Ten times more boring,' answered Mama.

Mama and Bridger had met towards the end of her final year at an inferior sort of Christian Institution about a thousand miles in every respect from *The* Christian Institution. Upon graduating she'd taken a job in a branch library in a city lying halfway between her home town and the place where Bridger dwelt. It was a boring, penny-pinching life but she was convinced that after a year or two 'out in the field' she would marry her Distinguished Man and never afterwards be obliged to think about her maintenance. It was what everyone who knew her expected. It was what the Distinguished Man himself expected – except that he expected her to marry some *other* distinguished man, preferably one with plenty of money. Bridger wanted Mama to have a comfortable life, with some social standing and scope for her talents as a cultivated amateur. Nor would it in any way harm The Christian Institution to have one more good friend with access to a substantial bank account. Bridger had always found wives and alumnae useful supplements to his millionaires, corporations and foundations. There was nothing cynical in the way Bridger made his kitchen garden grow. He genuinely liked the women he knew. He liked them for themselves. He took pleasure in their company and they took pleasure in his.

Mama's estimate of Mrs Bridger's prospect for a still more extended life, based upon the evidence of her handwriting ('Such a mother cannot be eternal!'), was both strengthened and undermined when on the appointed Friday afternoon in early December she met the dragon octogenarian. On the one hand the tiny old lady looked as alert and well as a yearling mamba. On the other hand she seemed always to be falling down and damaging herself. She might have one foot in plaster (as indeed she did have) but that foot was nowhere near the grave.

Some time after dinner that first evening Bridger's mother had excused herself and gone upstairs. Mama had assumed it was the old lady's bed-time. She therefore left her own chair and dared to place herself literally at Bridger's feet as he sat in front of the burning hickory logs in the music room. She had dared to lay her cheek upon his knee and give herself up entirely to a feeling of bliss. She imagined herself no longer a bud but a fully-opened flower. Whereupon Mrs Bridger had tipped over in the dark of the adjacent room and opened her scalp on the projecting corner of a bookcase. Her subsequent yips sounded to Mama like nothing human. At the first of them Bridger had shot off the sofa, almost thrusting Mama into the fire, and was down on his knees beside his shrieking mother before Mama was able to work out what the source of such uncivil sounds could possibly be. You felt, she said to someone later, it was the kind of thing that ought to be audible only to the ears of dogs.

Maud telephoned at once for an ambulance, while Bridger gathered his mother up and set her down in a huge leather club chair. Mama, hovering uselessly, noticed on the unplastered foot a bunion like a cherry tomato glowing through the tight grey stocking. She remembered what a drug store clerk had said to her once, for no reason at all. 'God, you have ugly feet! Do you lift weights?'

'I'm all right,' Mrs Bridger kept insisting, while Maud and Bridger sopped at the blood oozing between the lips of the cut and trickling among the roots of the tastefully dyed hair. 'I don't want an ambulance.' But when the ambulance arrived the old lady walked out unassisted and got in. Bridger and Maud accompanied her to the emergency ward. Mama, the superfluous guest, remained at the house entertaining some startling spontaneous feelings, not at all the sort any decent human being could admit to. They

were monstrous complaints, coarsely phrased and supported by the conviction that Mother Bridger had sneaked
back downstairs to spy on her boy and 'that girl'. Why else
would she have been creeping around the library in the
dark like that? 'The clumsy old bitch,' muttered Mama. 'If
nothing else, why can't she at least keep herself upright?
Why can't she use a stick? Or crutches. What if they
decided to keep her in the hospital? If they did that, Mama
would have to offer to leave in the morning and then God
alone knew when she'd ever see Bridger or this house
again; they lived so far apart in this enormous country.
'Oh the clumsy *bitch*!'

Mama sought to calm herself by reading Matthew
Arnold's literary essays, a copy of which Bridger had
plucked from a shelf and thrust into her hands as he was
leaving, saying that she should go upstairs and wait in the
little sitting room until he returned. An hour passed. Seven
stitches laced the widow's scalp but no drop of anesthetic
polluted her veins when she and Maud and Bridger came
back. Mrs Bridger was in fettle. Mama made a show of
relief and delight at her resilience while Maud and Bridger
described the amazement she had provoked amongst the
medical staff. 'This woman is purpose-built to survive
indefinitely and well beyond the lifespan of her only
begotten son,' thought Mama, who was finally beginning
to understand the problem.

The morning after her accident in the library Bridger's
mother stayed in bed with a headache but she was up for
lunch. In the afternoon, while Bridger was spending an
hour or two at his desk drafting an appeal to the alumni
for seven million dollars, Bridger's mother assured Mama
that Bridger would definitely marry her. She winked that
gentian eye and said, 'He talks about you all the time.'
Mama might still have believed this if she had not, to
climax the events of the previous night, already made her
conclusive mistake where Bridger was concerned.

It had been considerably after midnight when Bridger

had left Mama in the music room for the second time that evening and gone up to see how his mother was. When he'd come down again it was to report that she was asleep. Bridger had removed his shoes, carefully working the knots out of the laces, and after poking the fire, stretched himself on the sofa. He was feeling exhausted, but his duty (and his pleasure) as a host required him to spend a little more time in the company of his pretty guest on the evening of her arrival. How pretty she was in the fire-light. How very, very pretty!

Mama had resumed her place on the floor beside Bridger. They had lapsed into drowsy silence. It felt good to Bridger having Mama there beside him. He just loved to be near her like this, just quietly. He felt very comfortable with her. He even imagined himself saying to her sometime: 'If you haven't married anyone by the time you're thirty I just may marry you myself!' Mama had felt a bit depressed when she saw that Bridger seemed to be falling asleep on the sofa. His eyes had closed and his jaw was ajar so that his breathing grew noisy. In any other man the noise would have been described as a snore, but Mama could not accept that her beloved was a snoring man and she refused to take any notice. She wanted him to have his little nap, certainly. He needed it. But afterwards she wanted him to wake up and put his arms around her and talk intimately to her, telling her everything that he had done or thought about since the day he was born. She wanted to know him better than he knew himself, sharing all his experiences, all his ideas and his feelings. All his jokes and hopes. All his plans. She wanted to be just what he often told her she was, what he liked to call her: his pal. It wasn't a romantic kind of pet name – pal. It was the kind a fellow might like for his horse or his dog. But to Mama it signified something about her relationship with Bridger. It meant there was a lot more to it than just love and (potentially) sex. Or a lot more to love than just sex. Yes. That was *more* the way it was, for Mama had tried hard to assimilate all of

Bridger's attitudes. Sex was physical and therefore rather low; love was the Word Over All. Love was children. Bridger loved children. Or said that he did. Mama wasn't at all sure about herself but she guessed she'd like children if they were Bridger's children. Bridger, of all the men in the world, ought to have a son. As matters stood he was the very last of his line. This need not always be so. Mama gazed at him in the hot, flickery light. His life seemed so lonely and so nearly finished up. She could see now for herself that Bridger had everything a man could want except the one thing he should want most of all, the only thing she almost certainly could provide, the only immortality a man can ever really have.

'Darling,' she raised herself a little to get her eyes nearer his. 'Do you know what I want more than anything else in the world? I want,' she nearly whispered it, 'I want to give you a son.'

Bridger had to swim back to consciousness from the heat and muddle of his doze. 'What? What do you want?'

'I want to give you a son,' Mama repeated quickly in a still smaller voice and now she was smiling because she had begun to feel terribly embarrassed.

'Oh for Gad's sake!' Bridger sprang off the sofa as if he'd heard his mother howling again. He went off to the other end of the room and stood for a long time looking out at the snow-flecked campus elms through the panes of the French doors. He was astonished, first at the force of his feelings, then at the direction his thoughts veered in, for he had found himself irrelevantly reflecting that every one of those elms probably contained at least one fat, sleeping squirrel – Maud being the tireless philanthropist to birds and bushy-tailed rodents that she was, so that all summer long the campus swarmed with them. Finally Bridger returned to the sofa where Mama huddled, clenching her eyelids against her boiling tears. Bridger gently pulled her to her feet and made her stand facing him. He put his arms around her. 'I'm sorry,' he said. 'That was rude of me. But, pal, you mustn't wish things like that. You mustn't.'

'I'm sorry,' Mama smiled as hard as she could. 'I won't any more.' Then she slipped free of him and picked up a pillow from the sofa. 'Think fast!' she'd cried, flinging it at his head. They'd hurled the slow pillow to and fro, laughing and circling around and around the sofa. Mama had always been able to make Bridger laugh. But eventually he sat down again and pulled Mama on to his lap. 'Listen, pal, let's have a little talk. I have a birthday coming up in a couple of months. Do you know how old I'll be? I'll be fifty-three years old. In just another seven years I'll be sixty. Sixty years old, pal. I'll be an old man.' He had paused with his eyes swimming around in hers. 'And I don't *feel* like an old man – that's the pity of it.'

Mama clenched up again. Instead of feeling sorry for Bridger she was angry with him. He had made her feel just like a little ignorant girl being taken on to an elder's knee to receive An Explanation Of Life From The Acknowledged Highest Authority On The Subject Who Although He Believes The Child Is Still Too Young To Understand Nevertheless Recognizes That She Is Too Old Safely To Be Left In Ignorance. Bridger had given her a crushing hug and a dry peck on the lips. He had done this hastily, as if she were red-hot and burned him. Mama understood now that in Bridger's view she had become a sort of moth on the wall, a creature whose presence in his house was after all not quite desirable. Bridger understood that the considerate way to deal with a moth was to clap a glass over it, slide a card under it, and carry it to an external source of light. 'You'll find someone to love,' he told her. 'There's someone for you just around the corner.'

Mama had gone up to her room then with only that one thing clear in her mind. 'If Bridger and I were to describe, each in his own words, what life is, anyone listening would have to suppose that we were talking about entirely different things. It was almost like the difference between life and art, she thought. Like the difference between experiencing crucifixion and fervently reciting the Mass. Or maybe – could there be *two* Gods? One who cut out all the pieces and one who stuck them together and they hadn't worked to the same general plan?

Bridger, though he liked to refer to his 'so-called' mind nevertheless knew its value and took it seriously. It was the gift of God and must be returned to the Giver well-used. When Bridger came right down to it he agreed with Aquinas who agreed with Augustine that 'nothing so casts down the manly mind from its heights as the fondling of women.'

As for Mama she would learn eventually that what may appear in the night to be an opportunity disastrously lost turns out by morning to be a most blessed and narrow escape.

Wool

libraria -ae,f. (libra), a female who weighed out the wool to the slaves, Juv.

Mama had been looking up something else when she came upon this entry in Cassell's Latin Dictionary. 'A female who weighed out the wool to the slaves.' Mama repeated it several times with bitter satisfaction. A perfect description of her job in the Middens University Libraries, Downtown Campus, Reference Division.

Libraries! That pretension still nearly choked her. *Libraries* yet. Two floors of half-empty stacks at the top of what had been an honest commercial warehouse until it was acquired by a real estate speculator at his tax lawyer's behest and presented, with flourishes, to the borough authorities as the beginnings of a new private university – a university that a dozen years later still had next to no buildings (let alone any dreaming spires), no grounds and almost no entrance requirements. But as virtually all that was needed for admission was the ability to pay the fees it had plenty of students – from California, most of them.

A dark-eyed, good-looking Italian boy stood in Mama's office, batting his eyelashes and asking her where the Encyclopedia of the Social Sciences was.

'In the catalogue,' said Mama, glancing up and glancing down.

'In – the catalogue?' the boy repeated with charming confusion. 'But encyclopedias would probably be in here, wouldn't they?' He was insisting upon himself now, standing just in front of Mama's desk in his tight chinos.

'No,' said Mama. 'Not in here.'

'Over there?' He looked across the corridor at the Reserve and Periodicals counter, showing Mama his profile.

'No.'

'In there?'

'Yes. You'll notice the sign on the door: Reference Room.'

'Oh, yeah. Onna right side, honey, or left?'

'Go on,' said Mama. 'Explore. What's the number for social sciences?'

'Don't know.'

'Where would you go to find out?'

'Thought you could tell me, doll.'

'The library catalogue is the primary tool for the library user. At the beginning of the year you were instructed in the use of the catalogue. I instructed you. The catalogue has its anomalies, I agree, but the Encyclopedia of the Social Sciences is not amongst them. If you find the number you will find the volumes on the corresponding shelves.'

The pretty boy left the office sulkily. His girl friend had been waiting for him just outside the door. Politely she put her head in and spoke:

'In Israel, we have a different system,' she said. 'We tell the librarian what we need and *he* gets it *for* us.' She giggled. 'It's easier.'

'Do libraries in Israel have catalogues?' asked Mama.

'Oh yes.'

'Well then, that certainly *is* a different system.'

At first Middens University hadn't seemed so bad to Mama. Obviously the intellectual temperature of the whole institution was very low, but as far as the 'libraries' were concerned, at least, no efforts were being made to rouse them from dormancy in any of the conventional ways, such as the development of an orderly acquisitions policy or an informed and helpful staff or an adequate physical plant. There was little of that busywork that had haunted Mama in her previous jobs; that was, in fact, the spectre of her profession. At Middens she was not 'in charge' of any other workers and hadn't to invent things for them to do in case they started reading on the job, like Mama. But just let Mama pick up a professional journal and here's the first thing she sees: 'A librarian must choose whether she is to be a Cerberus, keeping all, frightening all, disappointing all and cancelling all of the cause to which she is devoted, or whether she is to be a Hebe, dispensing nectar and ambrosia to those who, by virtue of her ministrations shall become divine through her offices.'

Mercy! thought Mama. The notion that any student at Middens could become divine through her offices made her want to roll on the floor and slap her knees in helpless mirth. 'Wool to the flunking slaves,' she said.

Day and night Mama kept a simple, plainly lettered sign upon her office door. CLOSED, it read. Even when the door was open. And it was an incautious student who now appeared in that door – a large, genial, intelligent-looking boy.

'I've been asking around and no one seems to know anything–'

Mama interrupted him. 'My dear boy, congratulations. You have just formulated a fair summary of the general human condition.'

The boy looked at Mama blankly, then continued:

'I've been to all the desks and it's about Moulton – Moulton's Library of Literature.'

'Moulton's Library of Literary Criticism,' corrected Mama. 'A useful old work, as the title, correctly understood and the publication date accurately noted, imply. Have you looked it up in the catalogue?'

The boy looked embarrassed, then sceptical.

'No,' was all he said.

'Well, why don't you go do that,' suggested Mama gently. 'And close the door after you.'

It was one o'clock. Mama went down to the Faculty Club on the ground floor, meditating as she went the words of the spurious Enoch Sneed: 'I am so be-pestered by persons insinuating themselves into the Library to get books that frequently I am near to my Wit's end. There have been days when I was scarce able to read for two Hours consecutive without some Donkey breaking in upon my Peace.' Mama carried her tunafish sandwich and her paper cup of Coke back to her office. When she had first come to work at Middens she ate lunch in the Faculty Club, sitting alone at a small table, reading. But Palimede-like, male colleagues would approach her table and had they but known the passage, would certainly have cried: Come, shut up, shut up your book; the man's come who is to supply all your necessities.

Out of politeness Mama stopped reading if anyone sat down at her table, although her mind would keep muttering away: why if I might lunch with Marianne Moore should I lunch with you instead?

The talk in the Faculty Club was all of trivia and much of it was destructive gossip. Mama had nothing to say. She recognised of herself at least that she was poor at conversation. She was dull and shy and occupied herself at lunch in her own peculiar way partly out of these considerations. That, of course, was not all there was to it. She *preferred* the company of books.

One day the Dean of the Liberal Arts College saw Mama waiting for the elevator and reading a book as she waited. He twitted her:

'Every time I see you you're reading a book. At lunch, at your desk, in the elevator, *waiting* for the elevator – reading, reading, reading. Don't you like people?'

'There's a very great deal to read,' said Mama. 'Moreover, if a book is dull or unprofitable or silly you can shut it up and seek a better one without hurting anyone's feelings.'

Mama hadn't meant to say that but it had been so much on her mind that it had just tumbled out. Nor could she stop there.

'The book is not offended when it is set aside, whereas persons are. *I* am. And I'm sure, if it ever happened, *you* would be.'

Mama smiled brilliantly at the Dean. The elevator arrived and he did not join her in it. Mama, ascending alone, reflected that the time she wasted being delicate and tactful with people not worth her delicacy and tact was one of the most maddening things on earth. For his part, the Dean pictured Mama for a moment as he had first seen her some six months before: a voluptuous young woman, walking down the corridor towards the Circulation Desk, walking as though she balanced half the library collection on her head, her high-heeled black boots tapping the tiled floor briskly and in her hand a black book held across her breast like an emblem of state. Gorgeous, he'd thought. A well-stocked mind in a well-stacked body.

Mama poured the crushed ice from her Coke into the earth around the snake plant that lived in a pot on her desk. She took off her shoes and put her feet up next to the pot. Forty minutes remained of her lunch hour. Forty little units free from wool. She could hear students crossing back and forth in the corridor beyond her closed door, humming faintly or snapping their fingers as they went. Mama was so glad to be alone, free to yawn and stretch and crack her chewing gum and pick her nose and gnaw away her lipstick unobserved. She selected a book.

It was only ten minutes to two when she heard the voice of The Director of Libraries in the corridor, but Mama put on her shoes, spit out her chewing gum and opened her door for business. Two men were in the hall with Mr Greenfield. One of them was starting to hang an exhibition of photographs. Greenfield, himself a weekend painter, used the library halls to show the work of his Woodstocky friends. Art at Middens had never been quite so keenly studied as on the morning 'fuck you' was found scrawled in chalk across one of Greenfield's own canvases. Mr McGrew, the Night Librarian, had declared he thought Greenfield had put it there himself.

The other man with Greenfield marched into Mama's office as if it were his own. He was brisk, short, tight-skinned, tan, wearing a shaggy, ginger-coloured hat with the silver profile of a pointer pinned to the braided band, and he spoke in a high, hoarse voice.

'There a phone in here?'

Mama felt angry at first when she saw he was going to stay. He hung his coat across an overhead stack support, first placing a newspaper over the steel spar, and settled down to the contents of his olive leather attaché case. Mama noticed that the light where he was sitting was bad and as soon as she thought how hard that was going to be on his eyes if he stayed there she felt a little better about his staying there. At intervals of fifteen or twenty minutes he would telephone his broker. He didn't bother to lower his voice.

'Well, you got twenty minutes yet,' he told the broker at twenty minutes to three. At five minutes to three he took the telephone off the cradle and laid it on the desk.

'This is the one minute of the day you *gotta* be on the phone,' he said in a loud aside to Mama. Exactly at three he rang the broker.

'Anyone been playing up SOC? . . . What's it ticking? . . . Seven ticks it's closed. Sell 100 at 9 – or 8 and 7/8 and we'll about break even.'

Maybe now he would leave. The man with the exhibition of photographs was taking photographs of his photographs. He came backing through Mama's door, getting something into focus. With him was Mr Greenfield.

'I sold at eleven thirty nine and bought back at eleven six so at least we have that much,' the wheeler-dealer announced, collecting his coat and case. He had not taken off his hat.

'Pigs,' muttered Mama as they all strode away.

With the spurious Jared Bean, Mama believed that no politician, necromancer, quack, astrologer, charlatan, humbug, gamester, gypsy nor vagrant should be admitted to the Library; that the light-witted, the shallow, the base, the senile and the obscene should likewise be excluded. She even half-agreed that, as for women, 'You will make no error in excluding them altogether, even though by that Act it will befall that you should prohibit from entering some one of the Excellent Females who are distinguished by their Wit and Learning. There is little Chance that You or I, Sir, will ever see such an One.'

The other female professional librarian on the staff at Middens was the Cataloguer, Mabel Pearson. She was locally famous for having a 92-year-old living mother, about whom she talked obsessively and in terms that suggested a sort of rare, valuable and delicate antique such as one might acquire at auction. Miss Pearson had an eroded jawline, prominent teeth, a long nose, an even longer chin and unusually deep labial folds, into one of which was tucked, like an ornamental button, a flesh-coloured hairless wart. She wore girlish cotton print dresses that were too long in the skirt, rimless glasses and Red Cross shoes. Wispy greying hair was fussed into minute curls. She had absolutely no breasts, but was tiny-boned, short, with post-like legs merging into ankles of exactly the same circumference as her calves. Borne upon these she came now into Mama's office as though wading a strong tide. She had been assigned, she said, by the Middens Chapter president of the American Association of University Professors to pass around a notice of the next meeting to all the faculty. It was an important meeting: the new Chancellor was going to address it. Miss Pearson spoke with an accent that Mama had taken for southern until Miss Pearson said one day that she'd never been in the South and wondered what it was like. This notice to meet, said Miss Pearson, her voice a high and monotonous whine, was ordinary in every respect except that it invited 'all members of the faculty and administration' to attend. What worried Miss Pearson was what was meant by 'all administration'.

'You know, in some schools they mean the administrative staff and just anybody at all, and in others they mean only the administrative *heads*. Now, I'm not going to pass out any more of these notices until I find out exactly what is meant by "administration".'

Miss Pearson wanted to use Mama's telephone to call the president of the Middens Chapter. She wasn't going to use *her* telephone in the Catalogue Department and have all those people in there listening to what was meant by administration, no indeed. Miss Pearson looked sly as she mentioned 'all those listening ears' in her own department and she smiled conspiratorially at Mama.

'I'm just not going to pass out any more of these notices until I find out *exactly* what is meant by administration.'

Mama invented an errand for herself.

She wandered down to the Director of Libraries' office on the floor below. Middens University Libraries were administered in a strange and wonderful way. The staff was scarcely a learned company of bookmen-scholars but Milton Greenfield, the Director of Libraries, had seemed to Mama to be a man with a reasonable mind (whose limits,

of course, she had immediately set about charting).
Arthur Gully, The Assistant Director of Libraries, who also
functioned as Chief Reference Librarian (and as such was
Mama's immediate superior) was a former army sergeant
and he had a sergeant's manners in dealing with students;
but he did know his collection and Mama respected that.
Gully was tortured with anxiety lest someone try to
change something in his bailiwick. Mama's predecessor
had wanted to change a few things, Mabel Pearson said.

'She was a very good-looking girl, like you. And very,
very bright. Only she was nearly six feet tall. And she had
all kinds of ideas and made a lot of changes that upset Mr
Gully. Oh, there was quite a personality conflict there.'

Mama certainly didn't want to change anything. All
Mama ever wanted, as far as her job was concerned, was
to assure herself of an infinite supply of days after
tomorrow. Her philosophy of administration accorded
with Milton Greenfield's. He was not the kind of leader
who has to do everything himself, who stifles his staff. As
Greenfield's secretary admiringly put it to Mama once:
'Our boss doesn't do anything – he doesn't even know
what's going on. Oh, sure, I mean, he knows what's going
on, but you know . . . '

Mama knew, all right. Greenfield liked to tell her how
he'd never had any trouble being an administrator even
though he'd never been trained for it.

'There's nothing to it. For me it's always been easy.' He
settled back into his padded executive chair, stuffing his
pipe with Mixture 79. 'I just seem to have a knack for
it.'

Mama murmured that this was like hearing Rubinstein
say that the piano had always been easy to play.
Greenfield rose to this like a famished trout.

'Well, that's very interesting, you know, because I could
play too. I've never studied music but I took a Seashore test
once and it showed that I have this tremendous musical
ability.'

Greenfield described the test – how many hours it had taken, how it came in many different parts.

'I couldn't tell pitches or any of that stuff, but when it came to composition I was amazing. They'd play some melody, you know, and I could give it right back. I have a terrific capacity for composition. Always have. Painting, photography, letter-writing. That's partly why I'm so good at administration. I perceive the composition. I can organize it right away. I have this facility. Now, if my subordinates come to me with problems then I know they aren't capable. If they don't bother me, if they don't need me, everything's going well. Everything's working. Far as I'm concerned when I don't hear anything everything's okay. If there's trouble, if they start coming to me, I know there's incompetence. If I hear about it, I know the person on down the line isn't doing a good job.'

Greenfield wanted Mama to understand that he knew how to treat fakers and phonies, too.

'I was looking for a really top-notch, highly trained, highly qualified person for the job you have now. And some of the people who turned up! Or *didn't* turn up. A man calls me. I tell him not to call. I tell him to come in and if he doesn't want to come in to forget it. Don't call me, I said. People are lazy. Or stupid. I had a little girl fresh out of library school come in for the job I gave you and she was full of theories. I asked her this: "Do you know what you are?" I asked. "You are a bitch and we have enough bitches around here. We don't need you." It's the same thing, really, with the faculty. Last Friday's colloquium on The Two Cultures is a good example. It turned out to be a battle between the scientists and the humanists and they were fighting and warring and finally I had to step in and break it up by saying now look, you guys, you're just going around in circles. Just tell me the difference between this painting' (Greenfield turned his left palm up) 'and that painting.' (Greenfield gestured to his right). 'Just shut up about all this arguing and tell me the difference between these two paintings. And a colleague of mine who happened to be sitting beside me slapped me on the shoulder and he said "Greenfield, thanks. You've clarified the whole problem!" It was simple. I could see the composition. Now, what I called you in for. Arthur's going to be teaching some courses in the History Department next semester, so he won't be able to do much for us here in the library. You'll need to take over his responsibilities.'

Mama knew that in every range of stacks, in every workroom and reading room and office in the library there were staff members and student assistants chatting, sleeping or making out; using library equipment to type and copy friends' theses; stealing library materials. Everyone who worked in it abused the library (Mama included herself). Everyone always had. There would never be any changing this. Although discipline and standards were the very things that were needed, ranks would close firmly against anyone who tried to introduce them. Mama had no intention of trying. She knew well enough the demoralizing effect it would have on her to accept responsibilities she wouldn't or couldn't fulfil.

Mama had already received a contract for another year's employment at Middens but she had not yet signed it. After her chat with Greenfield she'd gone home and filed the contract down the incinerator. She would be paid on the old contract through August. After that she didn't know what she would do.

Sylvan McGrew, the Night Librarian, bellied in to Mama's office still wearing his black beret, whereby Mama knew it had gone 4.30. McGrew was an old, bald bachelor and a catalogue of the dead. He had been the only offspring of an Ohio mortician and it had left him with a unique understanding of cemeteries, obsequies, sepulture, burial customs, graves, crypts, headstones, vaults, tombs and monuments. Not only could he remember which famous dead were buried in what European cemeteries (he specialized in the dead of Europe) but he knew exactly which district of the necropolis each was buried in and who his neighbours were. He knew, moreover, where all the memorial statues and all the memorial fountains and all the memorial plaques were all around Paris and Rome and in every sort of lesser place. He could remember everyone inhumed in Westminster Abbey and the Latin on the tombstones. Even when travelling in America, a thing he had little taste for, McGrew was at pains to discover whether an eminent person might be interred in the local boneyard. He revealed to Mama that he had found the American sacrists generally less knowledgeable than their European counterparts and what had surprised Mama about that was to learn that cemeteries had curators at all.

Now Sylvan McGrew darted up to Mama, grinned, laid the back of his hand to one side of his lips and spoke in a low, swift, theatrical manner.

'Confucius say rape impossible; woman with dress up can run faster than man with pants down.'

He grinned again and dashed away. He was soon back, a man of entrances and exits.

'Listen,' he said. 'A graduate student told me this one last night. It's just about the dirtiest I've ever heard.' McGrew lowered his voice dramatically.

'There was a young man from Nantucket/Whose dick was so long he could suck it/ He said with a grin/As he came on his chin/If my ear were a cunt I could fuck it! As I say, just about the dirtiest I've heard, but it's clever, isn't it.'

'It scans,' said Mama soberly.

A lively, pretty student who had been in the stacks nearby leaned out.

'Hey, there's spark in the old plug yet!' she cried.

McGrew rushed away, giggling.

On at least one occasion in his life that Mama knew of, for he had told her about it repeatedly, Sylvan McGrew's obsession with monuments and his obsession with sexual innuendo had coincided. In Dublin in 1933 McGrew had found a schoolchild's notebook at the Nelson Monument. Only one sheet remained in it and scrawled there was a message: If you will let me do something to you tonight in bed in your bear skin I will give you ten shillings. Meet me tonight at the Nelson Monument.

Mama always had a hunch that McGrew himself had written that note – written it at least in his mind and addressed it to Agnes Gray, who he claimed had first brought sex to his attention without explaining to him what it was. Agnes Gray was the daughter of the McGrew family physician who lived across the street. Before she and Sylvan were old enough for school they had been playmates, until one day in the McGrew kitchen when Agnes took her pants down and asked Sylvan to touch the place they'd covered, while his mother and his father were in the parlour discussing the sale of some furniture to a Pennsylvania Dutchman named Lamp. Sylvan McGrew said he had no idea how it had happened or what was going on; he had just done what Agnes asked him to and suddenly there stood his father and his mother and Mr Lamp. His father had begun to beat him but Mr Lamp intervened.

'Don't whip the boy,' he'd said. 'He's innocent.'

The elder McGrew had turned on Agnes Gray, saying: 'Go home, you dirty little thing, and never come back here again' while Mrs McGrew sent her son off to wash his hands *thoroughly* although, said McGrew, he couldn't see why – they didn't look dirty. Some time later, after he had carefully considered all the implications of that mysterious scene in the kitchen, Sylvan had told his mother he would never marry Agnes Gray because she didn't have a pretty face. And with satisfaction sixty years later he liked to remind Mama that Agnes Gray had grown up into a homely old-maid schoolmarm and never had left Ohio.

Sometimes now Mama would take unofficial holidays.

One squally Wednesday she woke up and decided to have a day off. At noon her telephone rang. It was Rosen. He wanted to come uptown and see her.

Most of the real power at Middens University was concentrated in Rosen's hands, because Middens was the kind of school that is renowned for its basketball team and its course in Business Administration and this set the tone. The most important individual in a place like Middens is not the Chancellor nor any of the deans or professors. It is not even the basketball coach. (He's the *second* most important individual.) The most powerful and important person at Middens is the Director of Public Relations because he annually produces a potent work of fiction – the Middens University catalogue.

Rosen was just about the only man at Middens that Mama had any time for. Mama felt, believed, that New York men used women as if they were public conveniences. Rosen didn't seem to Mama like a New York man. Mama said if he wanted to come over he could, and presently he appeared, with flowers. Mama didn't know what to do with them. The only sort of vase she had was a little *papier maché* thing she'd bought herself six daisies in once – ages ago in another town.

She didn't know what kind of flowers these were Rosen had brought, but they were stemmy. They'd never fit into the *papier maché* vase without surgery.

'A Procrustean problem calls for a Procrustean solution!' she observed gaily to Rosen, who watched her cutting up his flowers. She stuck the amputees into the little vase and placed them on the piano. Rosen had to tell her not to put them there.

'Why don't you set them on the floor in front of the window? Flowers should be down,' he said.

So she put them down. And she smiled, to show how gracefully she could accept correction.

She wanted to get him a drink. She'd been saving the last of the good scotch – presumably for him. No one else ever

came around. Not even Rosen had ever come around
before. They had been meeting for months in his office,
where he had a leather sofa. She hadn't proper glasses, of
course. The eternal container problem. It would be such
a simple matter to buy half a dozen nice bar glasses and
save herself embarrassment. Simple as it would be to buy
a real vase and to learn a little bit about flowers.

She gave him the scotch in a juice glass. Well, only a
snob would object to drinking scotch from a juice glass –
she hoped. One thing she wouldn't do; she wouldn't
apologize for not having the proper glasses. Just let him
think it's one of those kooky things I can do in the security
of my complete self-possession. Yeah, sure. Maybe he'd see
a juice glass as a token of intimacy, as a way of saying to
him: darling, now you're one of the real insiders. So she put
the glass in his hand, leading his eyes with hers so that he
wouldn't look down at it yet. After all, he had come to kiss
her. That was the important thing. Just as the scotch of
good quality was the important thing and not the glass it
was in.

He had come to kiss her – and more if he could, though
he wouldn't insist. He wasn't pushy that way. Tasting of
cigarettes and whisky and pipe tobacco, feeling moist and
smooth and seeking, holding Mama as though she were a
child, he kissed her.

Her little breast was in the big warm cup of his hand –
her little breast for whose modest dimensions she normally
compensated with a good padded bra which she didn't
bother to wear at home. Again, Mama had the urge to
apologize for this and for all deficiencies. But she kept still.
For one thing, she didn't want him to know she ever felt
anything. Anything at all. She could take loving or leave
it. She could take Len Rosen or leave him. Nothing had any
hold on her. She smiled ruefully to herself as the thought
struck her that this was almost literally true.

Rosen liked small breasts. If they were bite-size, he said,
they were big enough. Appraising Mama now Rosen

reflected that she would look better in her clothes if she'd give up that damned padded bra for good. Right now, in just her skirt and shirt, she looked enchanting.

He slid his mouth away and put his cheek against her lips. He was going to say it now. Mama felt him draw breath and she had already imagined she'd heard him say I love you before the words began to form out of the whispers in her ear. Then it was all she could do not to laugh aloud. This traditional con, this etiquette-book phrase, this ancient password. She could just imagine it printed in a seducer's manual: *in an intimate moment always tell the lady (whoever she is) that you love her. This alone and unaided can turn an act of banditry into the supreme compliment.*

And of course for her part the lady is not to laugh or in any other way appear doubtful of her knight's sincerity at that particular moment. What she thinks later on is her own business.

Rosen had offered Mama the correct phrase. Now she must graciously accept it. And to be sure, oh, it was precisely what she longed to hear. If only it weren't in the same category as her own absent-minded morning greeting to the hall porter and the paper vendor. Mama wanted to be the only woman Rosen said this to, and she pretty well knew she wasn't. At first she had suspected him of being married. He lived out on Staten Island somewhere. But he never seemed to stay at home. He even came to the office on Saturdays. Lately she had begun to feel quite sure that he was single – divorced, widowed, a bachelor. But not married.

'Why don't you take off your clothes?' he said. 'It's easier.'

He began to undress. Of course I don't love you, he was thinking. But you have no way of knowing that. No way at all. He took off everything except a crew-necked tee shirt with little sleeves – the kind of thing Mama supposed husbands sat around the house in on summer Saturdays, watching television and drinking beer. The tee shirt, which unflatteringly emphasized Rosen's stubby neck, had a lot of holes in it – some of considerable size. He couldn't possibly have a wife and go around with holes like that in his underwear, thought Mama. He looked, suddenly, disreputable to her. He's got on his work clothes now, she thought. She was annoyed, having to undress herself. That ought to be part of the seduction. A kiss, a button; another kiss, another button, and so it should go. As a little protest she buttoned her silk shirt up to the neck after everthing else was off.

Mama's old sofa creaked under them like a rocker.

'This damn squeaky thing,' Rosen muttered.

Mama tried to move in a counter-rhythm to keep the sofa still, while Rosen sawed steadily on against her thighs. He hardly lost his breath, and after a little while he suddenly pulled away from her and grabbed for his shorts on the floor.

Yet what if he really *does* love me and only *says* he does because he can't think of any other way to put it? Mama wanted to be fair, and since for the past five minutes there hadn't been very much else to think about, she'd thought about Rosen's whispered words.

'How are *you*?' he was asking her now.

'Oh, I'm just fine.'

'Are you really?' He was nearly dressed again.

'May I?' He turned on the bathroom light and watched himself tie his tie. His curly hair was cut so short it never needed a comb. In no time, it seemed, he was ready to leave.

'More scotch?'

'You're *very* kind,' he said in his courtly way. 'But I have to get back to the office. Oh. First may I make one telephone call?'

'Certainly. The phone's in the bedroom.'

Mama heard him ask his secretary about the afternoon's appointments.

'I'll be back in an hour. Ask him to come in at four. *Or* five – it doesn't matter.'

He hung up. Rosen never finished a telephone conversation with an even remotely terminal word. Mama hated talking to him on telephones for that reason. He would just suddenly hang up, leaving her with static in her ear.

He came back into the living room, stoking his pipe.

'By the way, you wouldn't have a book of matches about that I might take? You would? You're *very* kind.' He smiled, his pipe clenched in his brown teeth. 'Will I see you tomorrow?'

'I'll be in the library as usual.'

'Stop by, will you?'

'Okay.'

He opened the door and started toward the elevator.

'Thanks for the flowers,' Mama called after him.

'My pleasure,' he said. The elevator received him and the door slid shut.

Mama put the pillows back on the sofa and carried the juice glass into the kitchen, setting it in the sink. The scotch bottle was empty – good thing he hadn't wanted more. Mama's cat, who had spent the amorous interlude in the bedroom closet, was out now nibbling at the flowers.

'Damn it, Jocasta. *Stop* that!'

Mama set the flowers back up on to the piano. They had looked ridiculous on the floor. She sat down and played through some seventeenth-century Italian airs and wondered at Rosen, coming so far for so little.

Early the following week Mama met Rosen's secretary in the university elevator, and she had a little blonde girl by the hand.

'Yours?' asked Mama. She always felt ill-at-ease with the secretary, who though very young was already married.

'Len's,' replied the secretary.

Mama betrayed nothing.

'I didn't know he had one *that* young,' she said.

'This is Kathy.' The secretary pushed the child forward.

'Hello, Kathy,' said Mama, getting off the elevator at a floor that was seven long flights of warehouse stairs below the library. She waved to the little silent girl.

'I'll see you later,' Mama said to the secretary. Then to herself climbing the stairs: – 'I did that very well. I really can think fast when I have to.'

For the next week or two Mama almost wished that she would run into Rosen again sometime, by accident, just so that she could say casually to him as she walked on by: 'I met Kathy the other day. She's adorable.'

Almost the last official thing that Mama did as a university librarian was to attend the 13th Annual Founders' Day Banquet – the founders being the real estate speculator and his wife. Each year they provided as venue for the event in their honour the Grand Ballroom in whichever of their midtown hotels was up for demolition at the time. Previously Mama had avoided Founders' Day Banquets, but when she knew she couldn't possibly be setting any sort of precedent for herself she agreed to attend the 13th.

'Think of it this way: it's a free meal,' said the Director of Libraries, who was capable of thinking that way most of the time. But Mama understood well enough that there is no such thing as a free meal.

An Assistant Professor of Chemistry had asked Mama to go with him to the banquet but she arrived alone. Mama was off men. When she found her place at Milton Greenfield's table everyone else was still at the bar, so Mama sat down to have a good look at the Grand Ballroom. She had never been in a grand ballroom before and she was disappointed. It was grand only in terms of the space it enclosed. Otherwise, even its vulgarity was timid. Dozens of tables filled the floor with pleasant white circles, but above them where a balcony extended around three sides of the room the railings were draped in dusty lengths of pink and cerise chiffon amongst which masses of tiny, nervous lights blinked irritably. The twelve chandeliers also were swathed in swags of pink chiffon, noticeably sooty. From each fixture radiated a squad of life-size gilt store-window mannequins. These lay prone in the ballroom's middle air within a network of supporting wires, like crashed acrobats. As nudes the mannequins were neuter; as human figures they were wholly unsensual; naked and neuter. And each of them wore, twisted around her thin, elongated, wide-spread arms, more sagging yards of smirched chiffon. 'What can they *be*?' wondered Mama. 'The pre-adolescent fantasies of an apprentice Fort Morgan department store window dresser interpreted in terms of a backstock warehouse let by a purveyor of theatrical gauze to the Imperial Russian Ballet? Giacometti cherubs? Starveling Watusi swan divers overtaken at apogee by rigor mortis?' Mama's speculations were cut short when the other guests, full of free Founders' Day scotch, came to the table and the Director of Libraries introduced everyone. Mama hadn't met any of the wives before but she knew who all the husbands were – except for a middle-aged novelist whose connection with Middens University went unexplained.

Before the banqueters could get down to the shrimp cocktails in front of them it appeared that God must be invoked. Who the hell is God, everyone seemed to be wondering as they all stared down into bowls of crushed ice and what looked like babies' fingers. 'Grant us, through the grifts of Thy Gace . . . ' spoonered an Episcopalian minister from the heights of the head table, and then it was announced that Dr Bloch of the Department of Modern Languages would sing. Dr Bloch, in a strapless green satin formal, appeared on the balcony with a three-piece student band. Her voice was one of those Jeanette MacDonald sopranos. When she sang a standard Forties ballad in her semi-classical style it tested the courtesy of a Sixties audience. There was an automatic spatter of clapping from the floor after the first number. The middle-aged novelist at Mama's table snorted loudly and demanded to know why people were applauding *that*. 'It stinks!' he declared. Mama, who had a secret touch of the Jeanette MacDonalds herself, wished him in hell. The rest seized on his remark as permission to contribute commentary of their own and no more was heard of Dr Bloch's songs at the Director of Libraries' table.

The Assistant to the Chancellor sat on Mama's right. He was a floridly handsome man who had not, at forty, the station in life he'd expected with his Princeton PhD. Tonight he seemed to be interested only in how many times he could (a) return to the bar, and (b) insert the word 'bullshit' into the general conversation. He was heady with success in both endeavours. Now he turned his attention to Mama.

'You're very pretty, don't you think so?'

'Mmm,' said Mama.

'You're silly to let them stick you away in that backwash of a library, you know. You'll never get anywhere there.'

Mama was very well aware of the disregard in which the administration held the library.

'I shouldn't have thought it was a backwash,' said Mama quietly.

Dr Robertson stared at Mama but her eye was on his tired-looking, sad, thin little wife who'd been placed between the kewpie-doll novelist and the Director of Libraries. They talked across her as if she didn't exist. Like most of the men Mama had met at Middens, Robertson seemed convinced that Mama concealed a secret life in the stacks and he was offended when she wouldn't discuss it. 'Why should you want to be a *librarian* when you could be making a wealthy marriage, for God's sake?'

'Why,' sighed Mama, 'should people always assume I'm holding out on them . . . '

' . . . while they're all trying to climb into bed with you?'

'I wish there were some wine,' said Mama.

'Well, do you really care?'

'Yes. I like wine with dinner.'

'You *do*?'

'Yes, I do.'

'You mean you have desires?'

'Thirsts, let us say.'

'You really do have desires, huh?'

'Oh, indeed.'

Robertson gave a vigorous Bronx cheer. 'Bullshit!' he cried.

Mama looked across at Mrs Robertson again. She was probably the same age as her husband but she was so reduced in misery that she seemed to be very old. Her few gestures were those of extreme age. She had pulled a black woollen stole across her thin shoulders. She clutched the two edges of this together in one hand and sat with the other in her lap, withdrawn into silence, waiting for the end.

'What's the matter,' Robertson pressed. 'Don't you like conversation?'

'Yes,' said Mama coolly.

'Bullshit! Why don't you ever have any then?'

'I would – if any were to be had.'

'Oh bullshit! Since the first day I met you I've noticed you never have anything to say. You just keep quiet. You wouldn't tell anyone what you're thinking, would you. You just babble on in clichés. You never say anything except in clichés. Like just now. You don't give even a few . . . ' (Robertson ignored the hiccup that briefly interrupted him) ' . . . few inches of yourself.'

'And I expect I know which particular inches you have in mind too,' thought Mama. She wondered what she could say to draw Mrs Robertson out. There seemed no alternative to a cheerful banality. Mama was attractive;

Mrs Robertson wasn't. In present company this fixed the gulf between them.

The Persistence of Rathbun

The First Piece

The medical library Mama ended up working in closed at noon on Christmas Eve. Mama went straight home and looked at the turkey. Then she bathed and lay down for a nap on the sofa. On the other side of the wall Mama's new neighbour, whose voice shrieked like a police siren, was showering abusive syllables.

'Why doncha LUV ME BETTUH, Joanie. I'm ya muthuh butcha treat me so bad.'

Mother and Joanie, thought Mama, your spoiled love diseases my walls; it infects my food; it contaminates my sleep. You are making me sick. Every Sunday afternoon your kind gathers at the shore in broken families to stone the sea. What will be carved on your headstones? 'She loved her Papagallos.' 'She was loyal to Mister Clean.'

Sound and solid tenements had been torn down to make the new building Mama lived in and its walls were of macerated Kleenex. When a door bell rang Mama could not be sure whether it was hers or the new neighbour's or the man's across the hall or the couple's at the end of the corridor but she pressed the buzzer down until she heard the front door crash shut four floors below. She released

her safety chain and stretched out again on the sofa, only
this time her upstage knee was fetchingly flexed. Soon she
could hear Rathbun thumping and rustling along the
corridor. There was a brief silence. His key engaged her
lock and he appeared at the door in his business suit and
bowler carrying two shopping bags.

'While I've still got my coat on is there anything you
need from the store?'

'No, I don't think so.'

'What about the trash? Can't I carry that down for
you?'

'I carried it down myself just a little while ago, thank
you. Now why don't you come in. Shut the door. Take off
your coat. And give me a kiss.'

'How about the liquor supply? Any of that Canadian
Club left?'

'A whole new bottle. I picked it up on my way home.'

'Did you bring up your mail?'

'Yes.'

'Leave anything at the laundry to be collected? No. The
cleaner's? No. Tomorrow's Christmas and the day after's
Sunday. It's now or next week. Better make absolutely
sure you won't be needing anything. Any shoes in the
repair shop?'

Rathbun stayed loitering in the door.

'What's the matter with you?'

'Nothing. Just a feeling I've forgotten something.'

'Jesus! The turkey!'

While Mama was out of the room Rathbun dragged a
Scotch pine in from the corridor and stuffed it into the coat
closet, but the tree put its fingers in the door so that it
wouldn't shut. Rathbun leaned against it and called out
to Mama.

'Hey! How's the bird?'

'Okay, I guess. I've never done a turkey before. You
know how I disapprove of pre-marital cooking. Anyway,

I've turned the oven off. Do you think it will be all right?'

'It will simmer in its own divine juices while we have something to drink.'

'Listen!' said Mama. 'I can smell forests!'

'You can?'

'Yes. Can't you? Pine trees.'

'I don't smell any pine trees.'

'*I* can. Very definitely. Like Yellowstone in summer. What's *that*?'

'What's what?'

'There's a tree in the closet! A Christmas tree! Oh, you dog! You've bought us a tree!'

'I thought you saw me bring it in.'

'No, I didn't. Oh, it's marvellous! It's beautiful!'

'If dinner can wait a bit we could decorate it now.'

'I haven't anything to decorate it with, Rathbun. I've never had a Christmas tree in New York before.'

'Try these then.'

Out of the shopping bags red and gold and blue satin balls, and miles of silver rain.

The Second Piece

Rathbun sent his secretary down for coffee and a danish while he made a personal call from his office on the 20th floor of the United States Cement Company Building.

'Listen, you beautiful creature, I'm not going to be able to see you this weekend. My parents are coming up from Pittsburgh to talk to Sandy and me about the chances of our getting a divorce. And then on Monday Sandy's mother is coming, so I'll have to be uptown that night too. I'm sorry, but I can't help it. I'll call you the first chance I get. And I'll be thinking about you, don't worry. Now, I've got to get back to making cement, so you be good, you beautiful creature. Love you.'

'I'll be good, Rathbun. Don't you worry. I'll be sitting right there by the phone.'

And the phone did not ring. For once not even Mama's parents called. On Monday after work Mama went to a double feature and forced herself to sit through it to the end. When she got back home she studied the telephone hard for a long time. Did it look as if it had been ringing? Were its cheerful red sides still a-tremble from some recent agitation of its bells? Was it febrile with a message that could change her whole life?

It would not say.

What was going on up there between Rathbun and his mother-in-law and his wife? Did she dare ring his number and pretend, if someone answered, it was wrong? No. For if Rathbun were to answer Mama couldn't trust herself not to speak.

The Third Piece

'Hi.'

'Hi.'

'How are you?'

'Fine and lonesome. How are you?'

'Fine and lonesome. What are you doing?'

'Oh, moping.'

'Moping? Why?'

'Because you aren't here.'

'You know I want to be.'

'Yes. Then why aren't you?'

'I will be – tomorrow night.'

'I'm not talking about tomorrow. I'm talking about tonight. Have they all gone away now?'

'Umm. Sandy and her mother kept me up until two-thirty. I didn't want to wake you.'

'You wouldn't have.'

'What are you wearing?'

'Nothing. What are you wearing?'

'A tee-shirt and boxer shorts. What did you do today?'

'Oh God. I spent all day researching a grant application. Dr Coldfinger's next project. Teaching rats to breathe water.'

'Breathe *water*?'

'He thinks the lungs of mammals can function reasonably well as gills if the water is saline and well-oxygenated. You can imagine the implications for undersea development: people just breathing the water instead of requiring tanks of air and everything. Do you realize it is often possible to resuscitate persons apparently drowned in sea water whereas the chances of reviving anyone who has breathed fresh water are not good at all?'

'Hmmm.'

'Do I make you sleepy?'

'Ummm.'

'All right. What are you eating?'

'Crackers.'

'Are you in bed?'

'Mmm-hmmm.'

'Light on?'

'Off.'

'What did you do today?'

'Oh God. Wrote memos, extrapolated, made cement . . . '

'Played executive.'

'Mmm. What have you been doing tonight besides moping?'

'Reading. I was going to shovel out the apartment after I'd had supper but while I was eating I began to read Blake. *Marriage of Heaven and Hell*. And I just kept on. "He who desires but acts not breeds pestilence".'

'What?'

'What what?'

'What did you just say about pestilence?'

'He who desires but acts not, breeds pestilence.'

'Oh.'

'I was quoting Blake.'

'I see.'

"Sooner murder an infant in its cradle than nurse unacted desires."

'Cut the crap, will you.'

'The crap is Blake. "You never know what is enough unless you know what is more than enough".'

"Enough! Or too much!"

'Very *good*! Why do you always pretend not to know anything?'

'Do I pretend not to know anything?'

'Yes. You're always saying you don't know anything, and then you turn out to know everything. Is that fair?'

'Since when do I know everything?'

'You know Blake. What do you know about divorce?'

'Ah, yes. Divorce. We'll have to talk about that.'

Rathbun's wife suddenly threw open his study door, spilling light in across the sofa Rathbun had made up into a bed.

'I'm on the phone, Sandra.'

'I thought so. What are you doing in here in the dark talking on the phone? Who are you talking on the phone *to*, as if I didn't know. Hello, Mama. You thieving bitch.'

'Hang on, Mama. Sandra, get out of here and shut the door.'

'I have a right to talk to my friends. Mama is one of my friends. She told you so herself. Didn't you, Mama. "I'm *Sandy*'s friend too. Now let's screw".'

'Go to bed, Sandra.'

'You talk such a lot these days about going to bed. "Mama and I sleep together. She asked me to tell you because she hates deceit." My God!'

Rathbun put the telephone down on the sofa and pushed Sandra firmly through the door. He wished the door locked. He leaned his weight against it.

'Mama, I'm going to have to hang up. I've got a problem here.'

'What's the matter with Sandy?'

'She's a little upset.'

'It sounded down here like she was *laughing*.'

'Never mind. So I'll see you tomorrow around six. Okay?'

Something heavy shattered against the other side of the door.

'What's that noise?'

'Nothing. You ready to turn in?'

'Hmmm.'

'Okay, you turn in now and I'll see you tomorrow night.'

On the other side of the door Sandra wrapped both hands around the neck of Rathbun's antique cut-crystal ship's decanter and smashed it over the door knob.

'I love you, you beautiful creature. Here's a kiss. But I've got to hang up.'

Rathbun pooched his lips out towards the telephone's plastic mouthpiece just as Sandra approached the study door, holding a bridge lamp for a battering ram.

'You hang up now. Good night.'

'Good night, Rathbun.'

Mama heard the bridge lamp crack against the door just before the telephone connection broke off. This relationship is doomed, thought Mama. But after that she avoided in her thoughts what her bones already knew.

The Fourth Piece

At one o'clock in the morning soon after the reconciliation of Rathbun and Sandra, Mama stood barefoot in the gravel on the roof of her building – an insignificant ledge on the Manhattan scale – watching for Perseides. The breezy night had cooled enough to chill her and the sky was clear enough for a few stars to show through the neon-stained air. Mama remembered the stars over Yellowstone and wished she might have stood bare-headed beneath the pelting lights of the primeval sky when Earth's only local illumination had been its rare, flickering aurora. Swarms of stars, then. The whole book of heaven. The brain of God laid bare.

Mama decided there was no useful discipline in resigning a human mind to the thoughtless ease of following orders, but she could not decide whether what she did to earn her rent was of the realm of matter or the realm of spirit. Time was her treasure. Should she squander the only wealth she owned on quotidian employment?

To Mama, adrift on a sidling planet that, listing, moves in circles, rudderless, the stars are the harbour lights of home. As a swimmer embraces the water, lying confidently down on the wave, so Mama embraced the universe.

A satellite lurched into view. It was only one of those wallowing home-made terrestrials. Nevertheless Mama watched it until it set behind the towers on Columbus Circle. She watched partly because it was brighter than anything else in the sky and partly because of the way it bobbed and wavered, as through deep water an unskilled swimmer moves.

In the end, thought Mama, we always manage to attract our own attention.

She went downstairs and signed two letters, one of resignation and one of acceptance.

The Fifth Piece

Surely it was a dog, thought Mama, chained to a stake, running in snow, who made the first perfect circle on earth.

Rathbun the Plowman, following one pale horse, carves

his fallow field. The crowd that has followed him flings small children under his horse's hooves. Mama says that if one asked him he would say he'd been quite willing to die but had been prevented by the shortage of transport and the brevity of the war.

The Sixth Piece

Amongst the duties assigned to Mama in her new job at the Polk Park Public Library was delivering books to house-bound persons in the town. The Misses Fellowman, a pair of able-bodied spinsters in their middle sixties, were on Mama's route. She couldn't think why. They lived not far from the library. She decided they had a taste for service. Mama made her first visit to them on a fine warm day in October.

'You must come in,' they said. It was to drink their tea and be questioned. 'Are you a Christian?'

'Yes,' said Mama for she knew she must. And in any case her parents had meant her to be.

'What do you believe?'

Oh-Oh.

'Well,' said Mama, 'I believe in doing all the good I can here in the world.' She reached for her bookbag to distract them with Literature, but they forestalled her.

'And of course you believe in God.'

'Of course.'

'And in Jesus Christ our Lord?'

Mama acted on a belated decision to be truthful. 'No,' she said, 'I'm afraid I haven't come to that yet.'

'Oh, you *must* believe that. The Bible *tells* us we must believe that. If you don't believe that you can't go to Heaven, and there are only two places you can go: Heaven and Hell. Are you prepared to die?'

Mama was twenty-seven years old and in superb health.

She was an excellent defensive driver with an unblemished eleven-year record and no automobile of her own. She was agile and alert at street crossings. She kept off step ladders, never waxed her floors and rarely flew anywhere. One of her grandfathers had been a nonagenarian. Mama hadn't been to a funeral in her life.

'No,' she said.

'You must be prepared,' said the elder Miss Fellowman. 'You don't know. You might die in five minutes. I'm ready to go any time.'

So was Mama. Though perhaps not so much ready to go as ready to leave this place.

'I don't think a lot about it,' she said, standing up.

'Jesus Christ died to save us. We were born full of sin. No one is good. We are all wicked. The love of God is the greatest love there is. Hallelujah! First He gave us the Law. Then He was lovely enough to give us His Son who died to save our souls.'

Her eyes, like those of her sister, were now full of tears, but she maintained firm control of herself and the topic of conversation.

'The Bible was written by God. God inspired the men who wrote it and every word in it is true. Hallelujah! Revelations tells us – in the last chapter, I believe – that at the time the world comes to an end there will be things happen which have never been before. Well – look around you! It's happening! These children, afraid of nothing and no one. Are you a Catholic?'

'No.'

'You know the Catholics have their own Bible. They take out and put in anything they please. It says in Revelations that woe to anyone who takes out or puts in anything. I was talking to a young man recently who said he was trying to find the middle way. I told him there was no middle way. There was Heaven and there was Hell. You won't go to Heaven if you're not prepared, if you don't believe in Jesus Christ our Lord. He said he knew that, but he wanted to find a middle way. I told him to quit looking for something that didn't exist. He said he knew I was right. If you find that wonderful love of God – far, far greater than the love of a boy and girl, you will be happy. Not that you aren't happy. You look happy. But you will be much happier still. I was talking to a Catholic man just this morning. He said he never worried about anything, ever in his life. He confessed to the priest. I told him the priest couldn't forgive him if he had done nothing against the priest. He said the priest prayed for him. I said I don't need anyone to pray for me. I can pray for myself because I am saved. Hallelujah!'

Miss Fellowman was too kindly, earnest, genteel and silly for Mama to argue with, even though Mama was curious to know how, in her undoubted purity, Miss Fellowman could so confidently compare the relative ecstacies of carnal and spiritual passion. It seemed better not to ask.

'I've told you how to have salvation and if you don't choose to take it you will go to Hell, but it won't be blood on my hands. I've told you The True Way.'

It was true what she said about her hands. They *were* bloodless. Thick and white, without visible evidence of veins or arteries – the pallor interrupted here and there with brown freckles like stains.

'Now if there was a fire in your house and you saved someone's life in that fire, you'd be the happiest person in the world, wouldn't you.'

Mama got as far as the front door before she said, 'I doubt whether I'd be any happier than the person whose life had been saved.'

'Oh, you'd be the happiest person in the world. That person who you'd saved would love you all the rest of his life. That's the way it is with God.'

The door had a big pane made of lacy frosted glass showing, enclosed in broad borders of long feathery forms like crystalline fossil leaves, the noble figure of a stag, and a lacy curtain hung across it. Mama turned the knob.

'Well, I'll be getting back to the library. Thank you for the tea.'

'Polk Park used to be very aristocratic. It's not that way anymore. You're new here, aren't you. Well, all kinds of foreigners have moved here now. The population's exploded. There are a lot more wealthy people now. It used to be that you had to have a dozen introductions here. You'd be introduced once and the next time they wouldn't even remember you.'

Mama pushed open the old-fashioned screen door on to the porch.

'Everybody builds ranch houses these days. I don't like the idea of having the kitchen in front and the parlour in back, do you? I think a lot of it is the ministers' fault. They don't preach that way any more. They just talk about daily topics. Oratory. Just showing how much they know. That's not doing the Lord's work.'

On the porch Mama asked the ladies whether there were any books they'd especially like to have next time. She had already started a list for them in her head. The first item on it was a nicely produced pamphlet called *Organizing Fire Prevention Week in Your Community*.

'Yes, there is,' said one of the sisters. 'That new book by Norman Vincent Peale. I don't remember what it's called. You know he's the President's spiritual advisor, don't you.'

'Yes. And do *you* know that studies have recently been published indicating that in both Nazi concentration camps and Korean and Chinese war prisons those POWs who held up best under torture and brain-washing seemed to be Jehovah's Witnesses? Others who made a good showing were Communists, criminals and priests.'

'Well, you see! It's those foreigners with their Popes and atheists. And that's another thing. There's a lot of Jews moving here.'

Mama plunged.

'Miss Fellowman, think: What unites this disparate lot of people? Is it not, surely, the fact that each of them has something for which he wants to live and behave in a particular way? Belief may be the key. But no one belief seems superior to any other for purposes of strong survival. From this point of view, at least, the Communist true believer is the equal of the convinced Catholic. In these studies no mention was made of Jews.'

Mama was off the porch and down the sidewalk before Miss Fellowman found her tongue again.

'Here! You've forgotten to take back our books that we've read.'

'Oh, that's all right,' Mama called from the staff car window. 'Just drop them off at the library next time you're passing by.'

The Seventh Piece

Mama thinks of herself as like water, taking the shape of whatever contains it and colour from its surroundings, being without form or colour of its own. Without a man the clear sense of herself as someone had drained away.

Mama lit a cigarette and laid it to burn on the edge of an ashtray in the deserted staff room. She sat perfectly still and watched the smoke spin up in the still air. Sometimes it twisted so fast it formed a tube. Sometimes it was a thin blue thread contracted into itself. Now again, broad and blurred, without edge anywhere and not blue but grey. Mama moved her arm slowly in the air and the smoke blossomed, drawing the current she had made into visibility, turning scrolls, making a pattern like an X-ray she'd seen once of someone's spinal column with the vertebrae outlined in that thin blue hard-edged line and inside it a filmy marrow. Now the smoke rippled into opacities like barium in a gut and twined out into fragrance that lasted a few minutes, then disappeared.

The cigarette shuddered and settled slightly to the left as the burning weights changed. Something that was a solid object was vanishing before her eyes. *Rathbun*, wrote Mama when the cigarette was finished, *come home*. She crossed this out and began a fresh sheet.

> *Dear Mom and Dad,*
>   *Once the week begins there aren't any seams in it to let out and I arrive at Friday night just hanging by a thread. There's certainly this to be said for towns as against cities: individual houses speak of individuals. I'm thinking of a certain red clapboard house I pass coming to work, with narrow windows in the form of pointed Gothic arches and white shutters on them. And spindles of what they call 'carpenter's lace' along the eaves of the front porch. Most houses here are old enough to have a front porch. Some have been glassed in, but mostly they're still screened or else just open to the air and there is generally a swing hung on chains from the ceiling. I've yet to see people swinging but they could if they wanted to. Most of the front yards support a bicycle or a red wagon. One has a dead Ford. The red clapboard house has a dreadful clam-shell and cobblestone flower pot up on a huge cobblestone pedestal.*

Rathbun, did you have a red, white and blue foxtail for the handle bar of your bicycle when you were an adolescent youth? Were you ever an adolescent youth, Rathbun?
    Strike that.

> *For five hundred miles in every direction the country lies flat. Nevertheless, every house that has been built in Polk Park in the last ten years*

> *has been a split-level ranch house. Bear in mind*
> *that split levels were originally designed for sites*
> *on steep slopes. When a prairie contractor seeks*
> *to adapt this fashion to his dead-level acres he*
> *produces something foully misconceived. This is*
> *his formula: take two cartons of differing size*
> *and contrasting materials. Drop one of them on*
> *to the other. The result duplicates precisely the*
> *effect made by the tornadoes of the region, with*
> *this difference: if a tornado lifts up your neigh-*
> *bour's house and slams it down on your roof you*
> *can cry 'Disaster!' and claim compensation. If*
> *your contractor does it, you pay him eighty*
> *thousand dollars and congratulate yourself. On*
> *the whole, I feel fortunate in finding this*
> *converted coach house to live in, even though*
> *in it I'm as lonely as the village idiot.*

Love? Don't mention that word to Mama. She says it sizzles in her ear like a roasting heart and makes her stomach ache.

The Eighth Piece

The discussion in the staff room was on passing kidney stones.

'They didn't operate,' said Miss Natterson in her high, unsupported voice. 'They're waiting for it to move, but it's so *big*.'

'I don't think it's going to move,' said Miss McHenry with a very positive inflection.

'It's left the kidney,' reported Ruth Flood from Circulation. 'They could have dissolved it in the kidney but now it's in the tube. That's what Florence told me this morning when she brought in Archie's overdues.'

'They have burrs. That's why they're so terribly painful.'

'No, they don't,' declared Miss McHenry and she was positive. 'It's the size of them. That's why they're so painful. I don't think it's going to move at all.'

There was a lot more of this. Mama went back to the Reference Room early, without finishing her sandwiches. Her suggestible kidneys ached like stones. In the Reference Room two boys from the junior high had a woman's magazine between them. They were turning the pages, pointing at things and snorting. They looked up when Mama came in. She went over to their table and said, 'If you have nothing to do, please don't do it here.'

The two boys gathered up their school books and went out, leaving the magazine on the table. Mama took it back to the rack but instead of putting it away she opened it at random. The words 'SEX' and 'MARRIAGE' leaped out. There were questions: is circumcision advisable? How does the embryo develop in the womb? Mama turned the page. Maternity fashions. A smock with brass buttons all down the front.

'Just what you'd want,' thought Mama. 'If you can't hide it, decorate it.'

The succeeding page urged you to use Tampax and have fun wherever you go and the back cover put the insidious question: Do *blondes* have more fun?

'I don't know,' muttered Mama. 'Do they use more Tampax?'

The Ninth Piece

After she had lived in Polk Park for a year Mama was in a poor state of spiritual health. She could not understand why nothing ever happened to her, for the major actions of her will were so buried, slow and circuitous that she was completely unaware of them. The physical manifestations of her spiritual condition were nagging complaints that involved the roots of her teeth, the intraphalangeal joints, post-nasal drip and bunions.

One summer evening Mama was standing at her window in full view of the busy street below the converted coach house, wearing only a pair of nylon tricot panties. The dense, semi-liquid sun was melting, spreading like a sticky sweet through the haze. Soon it would begin to get dark. The lights in the room behind her were on. From time to time a truck would pass, outlined in coloured lights like a ride at the fair. The traffic lights spelled out their common triad in a monotonous arpeggio. The streams of traffic stopped and started accordingly. The yellow neon sign down the street, shaped like a bent arrow, flashed on, drained away in a sequence of diminishing dots, disappeared entirely and flashed back to repeat itself without end or variation.

PARK   P-P-P-A-A-A-R-R-R-K-K-K   PARK

It was visually equivalent to a dripping faucet.

Mama had watched all this many times before. It was always exactly the same. Mama knew that she was visible from the street, that she could be seen in all the details of her body as easily as she could see the cigarette in the hand of the woman down there whose convertible had stopped at the traffic light. The woman's husband, or whoever it was sitting in the other seat, could have seen Mama watching them if he'd glanced up. He didn't. The car moved on and its place was taken by another car. The traffic moved and was replaced by traffic.

'The traffic is eternal,' said Mama. 'Innumerable individuals compose the traffic. Traffic requires a continuing supply of individuals, who exist to compose the traffic.'

She whirled around to confront the individuals whose existence composed the traffic of her fantasies.

'Yes, you may quote me,' she snapped at the reporter. 'That's what I said it for, you god-damned fool.'

Mama turned to the photographer who had just emerged from under his big black camera cloth with an upset expression on his face.

'Shoot it,' commanded Mama, who struck a provoking pose.

'Wouldn't you like to put on – uh – a bra or something first? Just a little something – uh – casual?' Thomas himself had on a celluloid collar and a vest but he had taken off his coat and rolled up the sleeves of his white shirt almost to the black elastic sleeve garters. He looked very warm indeed.

'No,' said Mama. 'Now take your damned photograph and clear out. I'm expecting a call any minute from Forest Lawn.'

'Mama, they'll never let me print this in *The Woman's Home Companion*,' cried Thomas in despair.

'Of course they won't,' said Mama brusquely. 'Here, Gertrude, let me see what you're going to say about me. "When we finally caught up with our glamorous quarry it was in her converted Polk Park coach house." Make that her *charmingly* converted Polk Park coach house. Mention the manger.'

'Right, Mama.'

'" . . . our glamorous quarry, etc., She was waiting for a fitting with her fashionable little shroud-maker, Ghool. While we ate our fruit soup she offered to tell us about men. 'Most men,' said Mama, 'are like those plaster manikins for modelling trousers in cheap shop windows: above the belt they don't even exist.' Mama has been working very hard on her new book, *The Prevention of Sex*, and she has just finished the first sentence. She says she doesn't mind if we quote it. 'Eros spelled backwards is sore.' Having written this much Mama is wondering whether she has not already gone too far. She worries about Chomskian deep structures, conceptual art, and her own intellectual integrity. She says she asks herself many times every day, 'Is the intellectually viable mother possible?"'

A secretary interrupted to tell Mama that her crypt was ready. Mama got up at once and went to the door where she paused, glancing insouciantly over her shoulder and allowing us to appreciate her long, bare back. The interview, it seemed, was over.

At that moment the French telephone began to ring. Mama's expression changed to rage. She snatched up the receiver and threw it on to the floor. Thomas and Gertrude could hear a man's voice saying 'Hello? Hello? Hello?' Mama pushed down the buttons that broke the connection. She was frowning horribly and staring at the floor. When she released the buttons the receiver, still lying on the carpet, began to buzz softly. Then it stopped buzzing and set up a miniature wail like a distant police ambulance. Apparently quite maddened by this, Mama attacked the telephone cord with a pair of draper's shears which she snatched from Ghool's reticule. It was all over in an instant. Mama put the dead telephone into a coat closet and shut the door.

'Remember,' she said to the children, 'neither of you has seen anything.'

She went back over to the window and began to twist languidly to the music that came up from a convertible waiting at the light.

The Tenth Piece

Mama had often wondered what sort of answers people got who placed those personal advertisements in the classified columns of literary weeklies, attesting to their creativity, resourcefulness, energy, intelligence, eagerness to do anything unusual anywhere in the world. She decided to find out. She composed the advertisement for herself so as to imply as much about her unique qualifications and personal charm as was possible without spending a whole lot of fifty cent words. Even so, Mama couldn't do herself justice for a penny under ten dollars.

In due course she received a voucher copy of the magazine in which her advertisement appeared. It had been a good deal edited. Not in such a way as to reduce the word count, of course; just the breadth of implication. This had been diminished by the alteration of certain key adjectives. Instead of being a 'decorative' young woman, for example, Mama came out a nondescript 'attractive'.

'"Attractive" is an adjective proper to fly-paper!' raged Mama when she saw it. Fifty cents just wasted.

That evening Mama and Thomas and Gertrude sat down to a supper of goat cheese and vegetable juice and Mama reflected on how she had spent ten dollars for an advertisement that rendered her virtually invisible. Who would ever answer it? Would *anyone* ever answer it? Did anyone require an attractive, literate nullity with degrees in English and Music and a wide range of interests? The classified columns were always full of such creatures, nearly all of them described as 'attractive' – although one or two would claim to be 'well hung'. Mama couldn't imagine what *that* was supposed to mean. Artists, perhaps. In galleries or museums.

Over the next two weeks Mama had letters from eight public libraries inviting her to inquire about 'junior staff positions with good opportunities for advancement'. Just what she was trying to get herself out of. But there was also a letter from the Puritania State Opera suggesting that she submit specimen synopses of the standard operas that would be suitable for reading, scene by scene, during the intervals in broadcast performances. Mama did this, taking care not to pitch the tone of her work too high for society or too low for the gods. The resulting sober, straightforward presentation of one ludicrous situation after another gained Mama a contract from the Puritanian government to supply synopses for every opera to be broadcast in the new season.

After that she and her children were able to live modestly in Puritania and from time to time Mama added a bit to her income by writing little stories. Her stories were all very short, owing no doubt to entrenched synoptic habits. She wrote:

The Eleventh Piece

RATHBUN AND THE INFRA-RED

All the rivers are red. The seas are red
and the clouds. The earth is red. The
trees put forth red leaves. The belly hair
of rabbits is red, and the broken-hinged
jaw of the dog. Red snow melts every
where the hanged man casts his shadow.

The deepest wells bring up red water in
violent hematemesis. Offshore the oil
rig gushes coffee-grounds material, foll
owed immediately by a lapse in the mach
inery. The bit stops miles deep. The
mechanics are puzzled. The rig hums
softly but it cannot move. The mechanics
are baffled. Vital signs have stabilized
but the bore cannot be brought back to
the surface.

*The bore cannot be brought back to the
surface.*

Someone suggests laparotomy. Rathbun
sneers. 'The contraindications are
clearly igneous,' he says. 'Varices.'
Murmuring, the mechanics around Rathbun
stand back while he strips. His sports

jacket in riding pink. His shirt of
flowered voile. His French cuffs. His
Countess Mara tie. Rathbun is getting
bigger, bronzier. Separated from his
oxblood alligator shoes he stands a full
inch taller. Where he walks he leaves
kidney-shaped footprints in the crimson
sand. Slowly they fill with Pirrametta
red.

Rathbun prises the lid from a drum of scar
let grease and smears himself. 'I'm going
down,' he says. 'Portocaval shunt.' Again
the mechanics, standing at a respectful
distance, murmur. They are protestants.
Rathbun is their leader. He speaks to them.
(All his life Rathbun has dreamed of ass
ailing a whole crowd of people). 'Men,'
he cries, 'shut the hell up.'

Rathbun is about to free the bore when
great dom overcomes him. The bore can
not be brought back to the surface. Nor
can Rathbun. The hell is shut up.
So is Rathbun.

The Twelfth Piece

Mama had grown up in dread of throwing anything away,
especially anything that was useless or broken or defective
or stale or worn out because she saw herself in every
discarded object. What compelled her to eat the last
biscuit in the box, or the last radish wilting in the bowl,
was compensatory sentimentality and not greed. But this
was a difficult motive to communicate, particularly as
Mama would rather be thought piggy than confess her real

reason for compulsively consuming last morsels. She knew that fellow-feeling for the unwanted would only be understood as a ludicrous excuse for eating more than anyone else, although Mama never ate a last bit of anything that anyone else, given the chance, would eat in her stead – as for example, the last remaining piece of superior fudge. Mama's concern was always for the stale bit of candy, the unsuccessful cookie, the mouldy heel of the loaf. Having made her decision to side with such things Mama felt compelled to stick by it, even though as time and the white meat passed her by she more and more craved the satisfaction of her true preferences. She had grown up into an unsociable creature, secretly resenting those bold and insensitive persons who immediately declare which portion they prefer and take it without any consideration for the feelings of whatever they leave behind.

Mama wasn't sure when all this business had started with her but it had been at a very early age. She seemed always to have felt this way. Perhaps, though, it had something to do with the popularity in her kindergarten of 'Farmer in the Dell' which was all to do with choosing and leaving out. Mama felt now – when she thought about it at all – that she had not often been chosen, that she had usually trudged with a few others round and round and round the growing crowd of her little elected peers who faced her smugly from inside the circle and this made Mama feel sad about herself. But Mama knew that, to be fair, she had felt queer and uncomfortable whenever she had been chosen to stand inside. She had wanted to be chosen, yet when she had been it was never really nice. If she was included she was ill at ease; if she was overlooked she might be sad, but at least she was easy. Nevertheless she went on wanting to be chosen.

Mama didn't accept this as having much to do with her close personal identification with the last of anything, though, when she would look at it and think: it feels bad.

It's got left. No one wanted it. Nor did it commend itself to Mama that an equally reasonable case could be made out for the imagined relief of the last morsel at having avoided, but for Mama, the common fate of morsels.

'Look, Mama, a left-over radish doesn't know it's left over, for heaven's sake,' said Gertrude.

'But *I* know it's left over. I am responsible for it, of course, only in so far as I *feel* responsible. But I do feel responsible. And I wish to God I didn't. I don't want the last damned radish.'

'Then what's the point of taking it,' cried Gertrude in exasperation.

'Here's the situation,' said Mama. 'There's this unwanted radish. All wilted. Dirty perhaps, with maybe a sore on it somewhere. And a long hairy root. Not its fault it's less appealing than a well-scrubbed, freshly trimmed radish lovingly carved to resemble a rose and served on a nice bed of lettuce.'

'But presumably insensate. Therefore indifferent to its condition,' insisted Gertrude. 'The radish is not suffering.'

'Ah, but do we *know* that? Do we really know anything whatsoever about the capacity of radishes to suffer? Surely, don't we prefer *not* to know? To assume simply that vegetables are as insensate as they seem? After all, when we deny creaturely feeling even to members of our own species, how much the more ready are we to refuse mercy towards rashies.'

'I would rather hear a horse fart,' said Thomas, 'than a conversation like this.'

'Let us assume for the moment, Mama,' said Gertrude, 'for the sake of the original argument, that you eat the last radish without really wanting to because you are convinced it feels bad about not being eaten. This is not, of course, appreciating that radish as it wants to be appreciated; that is, for its quite irresistible qualities. You say it knows you are only eating it because you feel sorry for it.'

'But think,' said Mama. 'Is there nothing compensatory in pity? In your misery you have wanted pity, yes? You have even envied misfortunates for having, if nothing else, at least a clear-cut claim upon the pity of others. To be felt sorry for is to have one's bad luck recognized for what it is by those who are not affected, and are quite free simply to look away. Why pretend to despise commiseration? Isn't it much worse to be ignored, or to have the injustice you suffer denied altogether – even to the extent that you are congratulated on your "good luck"? What is worse than the despair of denial, when others cheerfully assure you your pain isn't hurting you one bit.'

Mama glanced significantly at Gertrude.

'We have wandered from the point,' said Gertrude majestically. 'I want to get back to that radish. And don't smile, Thomas, and say "I'm sure you do".'

'Ah,' said Mama. 'Let me take this cookie. Here we have something seeking to be over-valued. A cookie – or me for wanting the cookie. The cookie, let us say, wants to be the consummately desirable cookie, the paragon. It wants to be absolutely top cookie. It can't bear what it suspects to be the truth about itself: that it is, in fact, just an ordinary cookie. Even perhaps a slightly off-putting cookie – with a burnt bottom, maybe, or a dog hair baked in. A cookie, in short, filled with vanity and self-regard, resentful of its ordinary condition, which is to be a cookie amongst cookies more or less indistinguishable from itself. A most overweening cookie! Because of this it lives in perpetual envy and discontent. Happiness avoids it forever. It gives pleasure to no one.'

'The struggle to become free – is the struggle – not to *struggle*,' said Thomas in what he seemed to believe was a summing-up.

'At one time or another *everything* seems to be true,' said Gertrude. 'Mama, a man in a frock coat is climbing up the drain. He's wearing a bowler hat and carrying, not without some difficulty, a rolled umbrella.'

'Offer him a cup of tea,' said Mama.

'Mama, he's handing up a note.'

'Read it, if you please,' said Mama.

'"Dear Lady in the Micro-Miniskirt: Please DO NOT BEND to tie your shoe at the top of the stair when I am still down at the bottom. Yours not at all truly, A Distressed Gentleman."'

'The poor sod,' said Mama.

While
Nancy Listened
on the Bed

This interview with the English novelist, Asa Huntley, was recorded earlier this year in America. Taking part were Cormorant Thorpe, Associate Professor of English at Mountain State College, and two of his students, Earl Gillette and Norman Nertz. The frequent lapses of attention are Mrs Huntley's.

Cormorant Thorpe: 'Hearing that Asa Huntley would be upstate teaching at the M.A.N. Writers Workshop for the last two weeks in March I rounded up Gillette and Nertz and we drove over and met Huntley and his American wife Nancy after a reading (by Gary Snyder) one chilly night. Huntley turned out to be a tall, powerfully-built man, bearded like a comet, who struck me as somewhat Tartar-looking with brown, slanty eyes. He was wearing a teddybear coat and a ponytail. After some drinks at the Workshop we all drove out to the S & H Sundowner Motor Inn, one of those faceless plastic places that now litter this country from sea to shining sea, where the Huntleys were *temporarily living. We pulled some chairs up around a "wood grain" plastic table with plastic mugs of instant coffee breathing damply into our faces and – while Nancy listened on the bed – talked into my Sony TC 120 until two in the morning. Unfortunately this print-out begins towards the end of track one. My [expletive deleted] wife inadvertently erased three-quarters of it when she recorded a session of the Ervin Committee for her tax avoidance class at Middens University.'*

HUNTLEY: . . . and he fatally confused what was possible with what was desirable. The mind's lust to know triumphed over life's right to continue.

NERTZ: Right. Sure. But the heroic had already gone out of human life by that time anyhow, hadn't it? So he was only –

HUNTLEY: He was only one more biological unit amongst all the others. Ordinary little people ineligible for tragedy, incapable of comedy. Breathing in, breathing out. Almost grudgingly.

THORPE: Asa, at the beginning of our discussion you accepted my suggestion that your style could be described as Eclectic Fragmentationalism. And you've also agreed with Earl here that all of life is based on thinly veiled fictional incident. Would you care to define the relationship between your style and this general concept of life?

HUNTLEY: Actually, that's always been very clear in my mind. The concept of life as fictive has made my style inevitable. What together they make possible is fiction without the distraction of plot.

THORPE: How often do you wish that you had written something slightly different from what you did? Does that happen much?

HUNTLEY: I think it's important that there should be different ways of interpreting something and that even the author can have more than one way of interpreting his own work. It keeps it alive for him.

GILLETTE: On the other hand, you know – like – salmon probably navigate by smell. I mean – you know – the home stream smells uniquely like the home stream. [Laughter]

NERTZ: Right. Sure.

HUNTLEY: That's very interesting if it's true.

nancy: . . . and there was that time we went into one of those wholesale food warehouses and bought a seven-pound tin of marmalade and for the next six weeks we ate marmalade chowder, stuffed marmalade cutlets, pickled marmalade, marmalade casserole, curried marmalade, Boston baked marmalade, fricassée of marmalade, French-fried marmalade, stewed marmalade, scrambled marmalade, shredded marmalade, marmalade strudel, marmalade fool, marmalade à la marmalade, and a great many pieces of toast and marmalade – particularly at breakfast-time and in between meals . . . Gibber, gibber, blah, yakkity-yak . . . And what about *you*, Mrs Huntley, what do *you* do? Oh, I breed resentments – but only as a hobby. Because I love my husband and therefore I cannot ever tell him the truth, because we cannot ever tell the truth to people we love because as soon as we talk to them we begin to use their own language and in their own language all the words mean what they want them to mean and so we are always saying what they want us to say. Who could understand it, such a situation! . . . as if the masculine mind rubbed one sere abstraction against another and the female mind excreted white gloss paint to spread evenly over the words . . . and yet I still do like the word 'marmalade' . . . When I was just a little girl growing up my favourite snack was bread and butter and sugar. . . . Ace said to me: we'll share our lives. You cook and I'll eat. Yes, he said, and why not?. . . . In an ideal world Ace would be eternally tumescent. Yes, and why not, he said. I'm a man now; I won't always be one. And there's no reply to

that. There's not a language in the human repertoire with
a reply to that. . . . And yet when that man is writing, he
cannot tolerate the least sign of another human life in the
house; if I chew, if I breathe, if I play a record or walk too
often across the floor above his head – every sound pierces
him. And he complains that companionship has gone out
of his life and that we might as well live apart. . . . I think
you could describe Norman's face over there as wedge-
shaped; very narrow in the jaw but tapering out (can
something taper out?) to a rather noble forehead. Cheeks
that cant in to the sharp angle made by his steeply rising
nose. A fluffy ball of red hair way up on the top of his head.
James Joyce glasses. Earl, on the other hand, still looks like
a premature baby – the squashed features, the protruding
eyes, the stunned mouth, absent chin. He has a desperate,
hiccuping, paroxysmal laugh, a pitted complexion and
the most beautiful camel-hair coat I've ever seen, which
he ill becomes and evidently never removes. . . . I was a
tomboy, of course, and I expected to become an opera
singer eventually. Pretty quickly, in fact. I was living at
the time with my parents in a very small town, which just
about provided me with the normal social repertoire of a
gorilla.

THORPE: Why did this change come about? In what
way?

HUNTLEY: It happened very naturally. All of my writing
is in some sense an effort to make myself 'come to'. You
know, so much in our culture conspires to keep us asleep
and dreaming. As truth so often does, it started as a joke
– jokes being one useful way we have of thinking about the
unthinkable. You say to yourself, well, of course it isn't so
– it's simply too ludicrous – but wouldn't it be fun to say
'What if'? What if it were so?

nancy: . . . and Professor Thorpe looks just as solemn and
alert as a cat confronting a switched-on vacuum cleaner
for the very first time. . . .

THORPE: Are there any American writers, contemporaries of yours, that you especially respect for their intelligence or style?

HUNTLEY: Some *South* American writers, yes. [Laughter] I was looking the other day at one of those academic literary reviews – I forget which university published it – and even at a fairly casual glance I was struck again by just how lubberly a lot of contemporary American prose is. I've been reading Thoreau recently. Again, not a great deal but enough to see plainly how good he is. At the risk of sounding chauvinistic I'll venture to say that's because Thoreau's models were largely British writers. And it's a fact, you know, that English children – the few of them who *do* get a thorough education – are seriously taught to write and speak their *burthtonge*. American children simply aren't. Nancy can tell you that apart from the odd book report in high school she was never asked to write at all until, all of a sudden, term papers were required in college and it came as rather a nasty surprise. You may know this from your own experience, as well. Look. Why should seventy-five per cent of *The New Yorker's* staff writers be British? Because they write much better English than anyone else, that's why.

THORPE: Sometimes I'm tempted to think that the last publicly articulate president of the United States was Harry S Truman. [Laughter]

nancy: ... why can't one just declare oneself a temporal bankrupt, cancel the letters one owes, and start all over again without an address book? Oh, Ace, love, your fingers are as long as a skeleton's. And is it any wonder, if you always feed as you fed tonight on a Dixie cup of California red and a little plate of rubble?. ... I'm becoming virtually certain now that Cormorant Thorpe is one of those professors with a wife who teaches tax avoidance and a theoretical book on the American novel in which he insists on an undoctrinaire approach – he wouldn't see anything doctrinaire about insisting. . . . why – *why* should my adriftness, my vertigo among other people, my tongue-tied condition make me feel so flummoxed? Why can't I just *be* Asa Huntley's half-witted wife? Who expects me to have my own bearings, anyway. . . . I was shocked by the English. They speak a secret language that mocks my stolid etymologies. They didn't mean to shock me. But what *do* you understand? they'd finally ask me, their large, intelligent eyes full of sincere perplexity at the one thing they don't know and cannot find out: what it is like to be a blunt-headed, slow American. I came disabled into their country, like someone who speaks only a little Lithuanian. If I were clearly deaf and dumb, or blind or maimed or even from Lithuania, they'd know what to do. There would be a department of the government, a league, a society to deal with me. But I *seem* normal. . . . how did I come to be able to ask 'Who am I?'. Or to know that the answer is 'She who thinks to ask'. No one ever taught me to think or to ask. Just to memorize. Just to answer 'true' or 'false'.

HUNTLEY: I'd say that Americans in general are not very much inclined to make verbal distinctions. There is a *difference* between the nation and the state. You confuse patriotism with loyalty to the government. It might be interesting to argue that what is behind the American indifference to verbal precision is the democratic social tradition. There *is* an American novelist I admire very much and that's John Updike and one of the things I admire him for is his attention. 'Precision is a function of attention, and attention is a function of concern.' That's Updike on Milton, but it might also be Updike on Updike.

nancy: . . . you can't say we haven't been pretty good at making distinctions between black and white, though, can you? Now where do you think we learned *that* from, Asa baby? Here's a pretty problem: how do you distinguish between discrimination and all the other distinctions? But let it pass (it usually does) because something else Americans can do, without thinking, is distinguish between young women and older women and discriminate against them all. . . . No doubt Professor Thorpe has a very glossy wife, expensively turned-out in the relaxed modern way with a tipped honey-blonde bob and a wardrobe of humble little Rykiel sweaters that speak a developed and hermetic language to *his* humble little Rykiel sweaters. (That's the New Elitism, folks: *you* quit talking and let your Rykiels commune. It will be to everyone's advantage including your own.) *But* Mrs Professor Thorpe will almost certainly be in her forties. *Not* a young woman – ergo, a write-off. . . . except that an original cashmere Rykiel has exactly the presence and meaning of – the velvets in the Van Eycks: money and the power of money. Just as money and the power of money is the meaning of the extensive real estate unrolling behind Gainsborough's ladies and gentlemen. Your virgin Orlon sixty-five per cent tri-acetate copy just can't compete, sweetie. It's, like, *rented*. Ah, well – the ironic message of my clothes, the layers of significance behind the subdued exterior, is only me. A standard body. Fashionable. Universal. Size 10 US, 12 GB, 40 EUR. Requires no special fittings at a couturier's atelier. How's that for a grand tour des hanches, hey? And the straightforward meaning of the jersey I inhabit most days is the bosom in the background. Look out they say, for sweaters that stand firmly on first principles, yet are capable of transmitting delicate emotional and intellectual messages – messages that are apparently contradictory, never exactly what they seem to be. . . .

HUNTLEY: . . . anyhow, as I was saying, it was a transplanted European who said that only the infinite diversity of clothes can give us the value of an unfathomable riddle. Nakedness says nothing about us.

nancy: Earl's coat says everything. . . . You lie in bed in the morning and think to yourself that today – starting from today – your life is going to be as simple as the cat's, and you get up and the first thing you have to do is put on some clothes and that is that so far as feline similitude goes. . . . I am also troubled by the absence of lust in myself. The apparently *total* absence – which makes life with a lusty man more difficult than it naturally ought to be. The period of my sexuality was brief, and being severely disciplined in the Presbyterian tradition it withered quickly away – the ideal state for dwelling in this world, we were taught. It's not. It's not.

HUNTLEY: Aren't we talking now about the difference between outlast and outlive? Couldn't we say, for example, that Keats out*lived* us all? In other words it's not a question of duration, but the quality of responsiveness.

THORPE: It seems to be a characteristic of a great many of the late nineteenth century writers in Europe – Ibsen and Chekhov and Shaw, just to name a few playwrights – to create characters that talked obsessively about Life and Happiness while rendering existence intolerable for everyone, including themselves, by their unbridled greed and selfishness.

HUNTLEY: I do think that as far as Britain is concerned the nineteenth century has a great deal to answer for, though not its writers in particular. I'm afraid I've formed the impression that Britain – England at least – is an exhausted nation. There is something absolutely played-out about England that hasn't to do with its general tattiness. Something is worn out in the people themselves. Maybe all that goes under the heading of The Industrial Revolution just did us in and bone-weariness has become part of our genetic inheritance. I don't *want* to feel this way about the country and it depresses me that I do. But I can give a very simple illustration. Nancy and I were driving around a bit in Europe last year and one day in

Belgium we passed through what looked like a very ordinary mining village. It was somewhere to the south of Liège. There was nothing much to the place. Basically it was just the one street lined with little brick terraced houses, two up and two down, very much like any pit village you'd find in County Durham. But it was coming on dusk and in one front room after another we could see the glitter of crystal chandeliers. Now the County Durham equivalent would be a sixty watt bulb hanging on a piece of flex.

THORPE: Wait a minute. Can you really equate national vitality with the general standard of living like that?

HUNTLEY: You can if you accept as I do that in an industrial society material standards reflect internal conditions.

nancy: . . . and the street cries we can still hear in England as rag-and-bone men ply the back lanes. HAHN-EE-MULS HIDES! HAHN-EE-MULS a high-pitched wail, each syllable drawn long HIDES! pitched down, yelped out. The crier appears in an old Sunday suit and a flat cloth cap pushing his echoes and his sideless cart. His thick fists grip the long wooden handles; the cart-bed tilts. Its only burden, a long slack gunny sack with a dire lump at the bottom. HAHN-EE-MULS. HIDES. In between cries, harsh coughing. . . . Sometimes we hear coal-sellers. COO-UL COO-UL an intermittent, hopeless shout for help without any urgency or terror left in it. COO-UL! Like some behindhand warning of a disaster that overtook us centuries ago. . . . Walls within walls within walls is England. Street cries. Covered markets. Raw meat hanging all day in the flies and the dirty air. A shambles. . . . FOR SALE! This hoarse crier *is* urgent, sounding more desperate and more breathless the nearer he approaches; SALE! more and more like a last, convincing shout for help.

THORPE: You have a theory about the course of human

life, Asa, that you express as 'whatever we can think of we can do', which can be interpreted as virtually utopian.

HUNTLEY: It can be interpreted in other ways too, of course.

THORPE: Yes, but it seems to me you intend it in a certain very positive sense. I was thinking, for instance, of what James Dickey has said – that with animals wish and fulfilment are simultaneous.

GILLETTE: Right. Like, have you ever seen a bird that couldn't land on a telephone wire?

HUNTLEY: Yes. A meadow lark whose feet were cut off in a mowing machine.

THORPE: The point I wanted to get at, Asa, was that this notion of 'whatever we can think of we can do' – which let me say I personally find tremendously appealing, tremendously *heartening*, and terribly rare among contemporary writers – is not implicit in your best-known books over here. The books that more or less (on the surface at least) limn out a standard life of twentieth-century man: the job, the boss, the wife, the kids, the affair, the insurance and the pre-need plot in the home-town boneyard – do they fit with your theory that fiction is predictive, that you write out of your imagination and then turn around and find it actually happening somewhere?

HUNTLEY: Oh, absolutely.

THORPE: These things are related? Do you see them as related?

HUNTLEY: Yes. You see, when I was a boy I used to turn pages for the organist at Sunday evening recitals from time to time. I'm not a musician, you understand, but I can read a score and I can turn pages and the only trick was to realize just how many bars ahead the organist was reading. I had to be ready to turn the page possibly four or even five bars before the last because he'd already read those, you see. I turned when his *eyes* said to; I paid no attention to what I was actually hearing at the moment. A musician performing is actually performing in his head. His hands just follow the details of his thoughts. The mind is always ahead of the hands. Always. If he's any kind of musician at all. I suppose it's a sort of programming, isn't it. That's what it really amounts to. Nancy could tell you. She used to study singing and what held her back was a habit she'd developed very early of listening to herself. She would cup her hands around her ears and listen to what had already happened instead of issuing mental instructions for her breath and larynx to follow. She'd more or less spontaneously produce sounds and then try to fix them up after they came out, when it was too late.

nancy: Oh shut up, Huntley. The glottis is raped by the breath whether in song or scream. In fact, it is by controlling her screams that the great soprano sings. . . . Oh, yes, I expected to enchant the whole world with my marvellous singing and all I could ever do was howl like a hound with his ears screwed backwards into his skull. In high school they just laughed at me. Especially when I sang in a foreign language. And I despised them for the hillbilly hard-rockers most of them were. But how I loved those lieder, those chansons! Not a word *meant* anything to me, of course, and they *did* sound ridiculous, coming out of my mouth, deformed as they were and devoid of conviction. My teachers didn't know any more about it than I did. None of them spoke, *used*, any language except American and Americans at that time, anyway, hadn't the imagination to conceive that the French language, for instance, could actually be used by a whole nation of serious men and women to exchange a pair of shoes or produce an opinion on the weather or express some half-inexpressible feeling. The French got their revenge on me the first time Ace and I were in Paris. We spent a day in the Louvre and finally I was bursting for a pee. I couldn't find Mesdames. Ace always says he has minimal French but he doesn't know what minimal French is. Truly minimal French is what *I* have. It's not that it's better than nothing – it *is* nothing. And not one official person that day would speak one single English word to us, although I'm sure any one of them could have. All their airy gestures and '*à droite*' and '*à gauche*' just led me on to more statues or paintings or tea rooms until I was convinced that the Louvre is the largest unplumbed building in the world. Finally I told Ace I was going to do it in the very next Greek urn we came to.

GILLETTE: I've been wanting to ask you, Asa, has it ever bothered you that writers are in, like, this difficult situation? I mean, it's different for them than other artists. I mean writers seem to be – well, I mean they *are* – like, limited – just to words. What I mean is – words are – you know – well, *everybody's* using words all the time. Like for everything. I mean, they're in the common domain, if you see what I mean.

HUNTLEY: That has never troubled me in the least.

NERTZ: Earl might be on to something there, though, Asa. After all, it was Hamlet himself who said 'Words, words, words'.

HUNTLEY: Hamlet himself is not a writer, if you remember. Hamlet is a character in a drama. That is to say, he is something composed entirely of words.

nancy: How glad I am, love, that your name is not Earl. So that I don't have to go around the house yelling 'Err-ull! Err-ull, honey – telephone!'

NERTZ: Yeah, that's right. Can't you just see it, though? The Bard pulls into a place like this for lunch some Tuesday, it's about twelve-thirty. He's just in time for the local Rotary Club meeting. So he goes in and he introduces himself, see. 'Hello, fellas,' he says. 'The name's Shake-speare. I'm in words.' [Laughter].

THORPE: Nancy, is there any more of that plastic coffee around?

NANCY: Yes, I think so.

NERTZ: Oh, right, Corm. Hand me the old pot there. I'll plug her in.

THORPE: Asa, I'm sorry they've seen fit to put you and Nancy into a place like this. They ought to have found you something on campus. But then what can you expect of plastic America? Every little wide place in the road has got at least one of these monstrosities now.

HUNTLEY: We're not offended. We find it very comfort-able, actually.

THORPE: Don't be polite. All this phoney Spanish decor. It's not so much the bad taste, even, as the total standardization, the absolute sterility, the utter lack of any distinction. Just to look at this place you wouldn't know which of the forty-eight contiguous states you were in. It's completely banal.

nancy: When you say BAYnl like that it sounds mis-spel-led. Which is it, anyway? Is it banal as in 'anal' or banal as in 'canal'? Anyway, what's wrong with it? In England you won't find any two hotel rooms just alike, I can assure you, nor anything as comfortable as this. Your ordinary British hotel room is a loony bin for mad furniture and I wouldn't give you a shilling's worth of artificial bul-rushes for the lot of it. Of course there are a few things that you can *almost* count on finding in all of them. Things like a deranged mattress restrained by damp sheets, a dummy central heating radiator, a carpet bearing cabbage roses and chain lightning yoked by violence together, vaguely Euclidian curtains in all the rest of the colours, one lumpy arm-chair covered in furious chintz, a dressing-table mirror that tilts forward to gaze obsessively at itself in the varnished seat of the vanity stool. Of course, you can force it to look up at *you* by stuffing one of your wellingtons into the hinge. There will almost definitely be a dusty plastic doily on the night table and a bud vase with a plastic bud in it. America hasn't got all the plastic in the world, you know. For illumination a bulb will dangle by a bit of purplish flex from a bakelite nipple in the middle of the ceiling and it will be shaded by a raffia mob-cap. The wallpaper will induce Meniére's Syndrome immediately. The toilet will be somewhere down a cold, dark corridor. There will be separate taps for the scalding and the chill and the bathwater will have to be coaxed out of the 'geezer' with shillings and a match. To judge by the indoor temperature uniformly maintained throughout you would think that every traveller in England was in constant danger of physical decomposition, and if one complains to the management one will be provided at bed-time with a nineteenth century stone hot water bottle resembling a 12-pound bomb and capable of scalding the callouses off a fell-walker's soles. How could anyone possibly complain of a king-size bed like this one I'm lolling upon now, listening to the philosophers over there, each in his comfortable chair, soothingly illuminated by soft lights? It's true that those larval white lamp shades don't seem ever so Spanish, but their nice wrought-iron bases do. The draperies are colourful but the monochrome carpet is positively self-effacing. What else to whinge about here? The Honeywell thermostatic controls for central heating and air conditioning? That's pretty miserable, all right. The colour television? The nifty little fridge for your orchids and salami? The adjoining marble bathroom? The endlessly gushing hot water? The efficient mixer taps? All of it a deliberately wretched and impersonal business. Not a bit home-like. There's not a week's supply of the *Guardian* drifting about, nor a single one of Ace's used socks, the smell of which would make a pig faint. What's wrong with a little impersonality, anyway? Who can really ask for more than a warm room, a comfortable bed and decor that doesn't deliver five hundred volts through each eye-hole.

THORPE: You mentioned Woolf. What do you feel about her?

HUNTLEY: That the muse is more likely to come in an expensive hotel room. If you furnish your mind properly you're more apt to be visited.

nancy: The humbugs bother me, flying around.

HUNTLEY: Thinking about my own books I find the parts tend to float about. I know where my memory, my invention, failed me when I was writing them. So that parts of a room, say, are described in solid detail, very full and clear, and then come gaps around the windows or the floor is missing. The trick, I suppose, is to keep the reader from noticing. She could *do* that.

nancy: . . . Gibber, gibber, blah, yakkity-yak. . . . Woman: certainly the most versatile, therefore perhaps the most valuable of the domestic animals. . . . The ability to endure monotony is said to be a feminine characteristic. . . . What I miss, of course, are the quilting bees, lending a hand at shearing time and harvest, taking the cousins down to the river to pound a week's washing on the rocks, getting up round dances and singing-schools, putting dinner on the table for eighteen hands at haying. . . . sometimes in America now I have this recurring dream, in which mythic figures from Madison Avenue turn against me, personally. The Jolly Green Giant pelts me with corn niblets and attempts to impale me on a spear of asparagus, but at the very last moment I am spared, so that I can become, instead, the victim of a ceramic salt and pepper shaker, said to be very popular now in San Francisco, that takes the form of a nude with rhinestone nipples. She lies on her back on the dining room table, with her legs flexed and pressed together. The salt and pepper are contained in lift-out breasts that fit into sockets on her thorax. Her expression is vexed, as though too much weighed upon her.

GILLETTE: *Lunes* – that's your latest, right? Well, I thought – Wow! Massive! It's like the eighteenth century, you know? The virtuosity and everything. But, frankly, it didn't seem like it was *about* anything.

HUNTLEY: I want to defend that book and I disagree with you about the content. *Lunes* is about a woman in a prison, perfecting her calligraphy and then using it to write petitions for her release.

GILLETTE: Oh sure, I see that. But –

NERTZ: Yes, but then if you look at the character of Lila, her two greatest assets are always right out there in front. You can't ever get past those!

HUNTLEY: Neither can *she*, of course.

nancy: . . . and so many women go on growing as they age. I mean *physically* growing. Until we get these enormous old ladies, heavy as lorries. . . . and why should it bug me that Thorpe keeps touching that undisciplined moustache of his every five minutes as if to be sure it's still there? Ace is rubbing his cheek with the palm of his hand a lot. A sign of impatience. He has such long fingers. They're like roots. . . .

THORPE: And yet what about the passage in the 'kitchen prisoners' section where she says 'Consider my disadvantages: I came of age in the Fifties. I matured early under the First Eisenhower Administration. Have mercy.'

nancy: Almost without realizing it I used to depend absolutely on the feeling I'd always had, that somewhere off in the future – but not too far off – was this marvellous surprise, this terrific *gift*, coming towards me in the form of a perfect husband who would immediately recognize me as the woman he'd been searching for all his life. From that moment on, no matter what I did that was silly, he'd faithfully adore me. He'd be moderately rich and discreetly famous and I'd have a big, white, church wedding that would cost more than a college education. It was the bourgeois apotheosis. And everyone I'd ever known from the time I was a little girl would be there, smiling with an equal mixture of envy and pleasure. I'd be in clover for nothing more than just being myself. I went right through my twenties that way, being nasty to all kinds of nice young men.

THORPE: Can we go back just a moment to your very first book, *The Passages?*

HUNTLEY: Yes, I really ought to have put a note at the beginning of that one. 'Symbols explained at back of book.'

NERTZ: Hey, let me read the opening paragraph, because I think that's the whole book, really, in microcosm. I *love* this. Listen. 'It's been said of the world that it has no genius to spare, but in Manhattan that's a lie. Any dawn if you listen you can hear precious small bones cracking their splints and swelling to scar-tissued spatulates all up and down Lenox Avenue. At any time of day wherever you are with the ferrule of your rolled umbrella you can pick off a painter's eye. Magniloquent actors take routine calls at J. Walter Thompson. Heldentenors drive your taxis. Whenever you lurch in the aisle of a No. 5 bus one of your fashionable spike heels drives itself through a dancer's metatarsal and every time you squeeze into a seat on the BMT you crush the left hand of a child Heifitz under the bones of your gross buttocks. And it's okay. It's just one of those things that happens in crowds. And still the genius queue stretches from the Upper Bronx to West Boondock, a tail without a head, and if you are a genius you have to go and stand in it sooner or later and hear The Interviewer say he can't use no geniuses. "We lookin' fast typists, keypunch operators, file clerks, janitors, switchboard dollies nine to five no skills so howabout it Kiddo whaddayasay." And finally Kiddo puts on the white cotton gloves and runs an elevator at Abraham & Straus up and down all day, stopping at all floors, opening and closing the brass safety grill every time. But in his mind he rinses his drab car with silver and makes it a moon machine and a ship to the stars. When he goes home at night his arm's too sore to take up a slide rule. His hand won't grip a pencil. But his imagination opens up the roof of that department store as if it were a can of contaminated tuna and he flies out through it in his steeple-shaped rocket, eludes the fist of gravity and hurtles free.'

HUNTLEY: I'm told that in the early days of the automobile people used to believe that to go rushing along at 30 miles per hour would cause insanity. And sure enough . . . . [Laughter]

THORPE: Stanley Elkin has it that madness is the common cold of the emotions. I find it very interesting, by the way, that madness doesn't figure to any extent in your work. Your material is frequently childhood, dreams, fantasies, fugitive thoughts – in other words, the Id's devices for sneaking back from banishment, its hole in the Garden hedge. This is certainly the case in *The Passages*, wouldn't you say? And of course the strenuous effort at self-knowledge that the protagonist Kiddo makes is wholly successful in the end. I happen to think the book clearly re-affirms and re-establishes the individual as the basic unit of value in society, but I wonder whether any of this is what you yourself feel?

HUNTLEY: I'll answer that in a moment, but first I want to say that there's a bit in one of Keats's letters to his brother in America that I always read with immense refreshment in these times when madness in artists seems to lend special credence to their work – or if not credence, then certainly *interest*. 'I went to bed,' Keats wrote, 'and enjoyed uninterrupted sleep: sane I went to bed, and sane

I arose.' And we don't have to take his word for it. We have the evidence of the poems. The true measure of the intellect is the product thereof – which is why, I suspect, Mensa isn't more of a force in our society. But you spoke a moment ago about the Garden. I think by this time we have to accept that we live in a morally incomprehensible universe. I think we have to accept that Milton has failed – not as a writer, but as an apologist for God. The question then arises why, if Milton's cosmology is only a brilliant invention, do so many of us still seriously read *Paradise Lost*? I suspect the answer to that would vindicate my ideas about the fictive nature of life.

THORPE: Eclectic Fragmentationalism isn't exactly the first term that springs to mind as a description of the Miltonic style!

HUNTLEY: No, indeed. Although there's a case to be put for it, but that's another argument entirely. To continue with my point, would Milton *still* have written *Paradise Lost* even if he had *not* felt totally committed to the Puritan theology? And of course I say without hesitation that he *would* have.

THORPE: Assuming you're right, would it have been the same *poem* that we read today?

NERTZ: Right! Because what *is* the poem that we read today?

HUNTLEY: Are you asking would the text we read today be the same *text* Milton published in 1667 or whenever? Is that what you mean?

THORPE: Norman's saying that the reader in reading a text changes it. [Inaudible sounds from Nertz]

HUNTLEY: Well, then I'm saying *more* than that.

nancy: ... clear winter weekend afternoons when the shadows came out and the light began to wither on the snow and the sun appeared in the upper windows of the house across the field like a fire raging in the attic there, the woman watching from her own window began quietly to weep and she continued until it was dark. The cat beside her chair, whose coat was designed by the light and the shadow, who was as soft as flour, as soft as dust, wheezed rhythmically in its sleep, forcing her to notice that the animal was ageing, that it was now thirteen years old. The cat, too, was a creature that liked to establish limits for itself, preferring a box just a bit too small for it so that it slept curled around its involuntary smile, the four paws all jumbled together with the flexible ears and the whiskers, the eyes sewn down tight as seams.

Beautiful weeds like a thousand pencil strokes rose out of the snow on the slope up to the trees at the edge of the woman's lawn. At three, shadows that doubled the stalks had been sharp and brilliantly blue, but they had soon disappeared and for more than a quarter of an hour everything showed as of equal value in the pellucid grey tonality, in the perfectly democratic light. As the woman went on weeping the second half of the hour the light purified and collected on the tin roof of a farm shed down the road, under great black oaks ermined with snow. Everything before her was a pattern of man-made lines among the natural curves fixed in the straight, low light falling across space from far out beyond the limits of the earth. She drank that plasma, the snowy blood. Every weekend she got weeping drunk on it, sitting in her window.

A fly that had been fumbling at the pane in the winter sun lurched across the carpet, sleepy with death but stubborn as a child at bed-time, dragging out into the middle of January its disagreement with the laws of nature. The cat had watched it now and then, had occasionally cold-nosed it up the leg of the sofa, but had never sought to harm it. Now in its box the cat stood up and stretched itself. It yawned. The hinges of its head gaped. Its teeth clashed together and saliva snapped in its mouth. The cat took notice of the fly, and ate it.

Outside not even a string on the willow tree moved in the frozen air. Today no one else was at home in the few nearby houses. The windows in the bright walls showed dark daytime interiors, rooms not warmed by human flesh. If the young couple next door should come home now the woman's heart would utterly dissolve. The warmest lights in the world shone out of their windows. All winter they lived in cubes of amber light. It made the woman feel lonely, seeing that light, as nothing else could except the dying of the brief, bright afternoon. This was heaviness. Everything in the world married, the sky to the spotted earth, the snow to the tree.

To weep exercised the pain and relieved the stiffness of the silence. When the woman had wept for an hour and more blue was seeping up out of everything, substance of a dark plutonic deity. Only the seam at the rim of the world showed a fleshy pink. The woman's own interior walls and lamplight began to appear out in the snow and the little swollen eyes she was staring through stared back out of the face forming there. Darkness was bringing her home.

In the previous day's post had been a letter from a man she couldn't identify. The correspondent, who said his name was Greedyheart, claimed to know very well who the woman was. He knew, he said, her name, her birthday, her height, shirt size, eye colour and favourite vegetable. He wrote: 'Your hazel eyes speak compassionately for salesgirls and labouring men and all broken talents slowly dying. Beautifully young, you are stiff with wisdom. I see you as part of the detail of my world. How many times I have begun a letter only to stop before the first word had dried. I wish you were watching. What you would see is the essence of a conscious self. I have not had a letter for days.'

The young neighbours, to whom she had never spoken,

with whom she had never exchanged so much as one single word, had still not returned to shine their vivid lights on her. She would draw her curtains against them now, before they could. The next five afternoons would pass beneath the cold fluorescence of a public building, the woman's tears sapped in draughty labour and routine busyness. . . .

THORPE: Asa, I keep returning to your fundamental affirmativeness. It's something that lies so much athwart the central tradition in modern literature.

HUNTLEY: But my affirmativeness is not the same thing as optimism. I don't know how generally people are aware of this but at the beginning of this century nobody needed a passport in order to travel abroad. Anyone who could pay the passage or buy the ticket could go anywhere in the world. Except, I think, for Turkey and Russia. Travel in those countries was somehow restricted. But otherwise one could come and go in the world as he fancied or as he could afford to. Today the doors of virtually every nation on earth are locked. More and more countries are nothing better than vast penitentiaries, the countryside around the borders shaved clean, savagely sterilized and mercilessly guarded with barbed wire, gun-towers and searchlights, citizen prepared to fire upon citizen. People can't go in because they don't have the *papers* and very few can get out, for the same reason. What is the people's crime? How have these millions sinned?

nancy: Remember the story my brother told us? He was riding his trail bike in the woods way up in the Cascades somewhere, in a national park, and he pulled up to look at the map and some guy in uniform walked out of the trees and checked his license plate and asked him pretty accusingly where he had come from and what he was doing there. It turned out this Mountie-type was just trying to track down someone who'd dumped a load of rubbish up on the road, but my brother said that it sure seemed odd to be a hundred miles from nowhere and have a uniformed man suddenly coming out of the brush and demanding to know your business. You said you'd thought at the time, 'It's not odd.' Or rather, 'Yes, it *ought* to be odd, but there are not many places in the world today where it *is* odd and it's going to get less and less odd over here in America because men in uniform with uniform heads and the legal right to ask you your business at any time of day or night are the natural consequences of the authoritarian law-and-order views your brother is always pushing. . . . ' Wouldn't it be a good question for all planners and legislators and plain citizens to ask themselves, whenever they want another law, what would the ultimate effect of it be upon the soul and spirit of man?

HUNTLEY: What do all these Americans go to England to see? Brutal castles and vulgar palaces. Places where people have died. The more horribly the better. I've seen coach-loads of little school-children out on day-trips being infected with all the received attitudes towards historical sites – these are little *British* children I'm talking about now. They get taken, let's say, to Flodden Field, primed with a little slanted information, much in the same way that they are sent off to church. They come, they see, they 'empathise' and then they go home and write a little poem about how they felt at Flodden Field on the 29th of March in this year of Our Lord. And heaven help them if they didn't 'get a feeling' – or if it wasn't considered 'appropriate' for their wretched little knee-jerk school reports. 'Get a feeling'! Christ! Get your vicarious death in battle and your good mark all in one. In my writing I do try to say, a lot of the time, look at how much *isn't* here. The famous battlefield remains a field. Sheep live on it. The grass that grows there is just grass. It comes and it withers and it goes. It drinks rain, not blood. I did not die here and neither did you. And why, I want to know, should anyone. History is useless to us except as an educator, which is really to say that history is useless because we don't make use of it. What we do with history is reduce it to a subject for small-talk, sport, entertainment, sentimental day-trips. Then we somehow feel entitled to cry out 'We were there! We were on all the sides! We have died all the deaths!' For us the beauty of history is that it gives us a real place for self-regarding play instead of true ground for self-correction.

NERTZ: It sounds to me like you're saying all Americans are violent and stupid.

HUNTLEY: No, I'm saying that America is where all the wars in the world go to fight on into the third and fourth generation. I'm also saying the British can be cruel and stupid. England is said to be filled with animal-lovers and yet it's a country where dogs are hung by the neck and kittens are beheaded. I'm talking about western man and his appetites and rationalizations. About the thousands of sheep in the loading pens on the quay at Lerwick in September waiting to be driven up a ramp into the hold of the steamship St Clair and taken to the Aberdeen slaughter-houses and knocked on the head and cut into Sunday joints. I've seen sheep packed so tight on that quay that they form a living carpet over it and the air itself shakes and pants above their heaving pelts. You can hear their terror. It makes a sound like the idling of an ill-adjusted motor. Shuddering, quivering. The black faces and the white sweating with terror. And you know that their lives will continue for a day or two without food or space or light and end in this unabating terror some kneel in already, though there is no room to kneel. But they will never eat heather on Aithsting again, nor shelter from the gale in the peaty banks of Reawick. So neither of us ever eats what's been slaughtered. And so what. So what.

nancy: There is a fine polished red granite drinking fountain beside the quay at Lerwick with an incised and gilded inscription that says 'I shall trust and not be afraid'. Perhaps it was intended for horses.

HUNTLEY: You see, once we become conscious of something, whatever it is, we are inevitably changed. We don't have to *do* anything about that. And usually we don't. Not until we are compelled to. It changes us, though, all the same. It doesn't wait on us. Perhaps human fate is meant to be deeply unnatural. Or maybe it's only meant to be irreconcilably divided.

nancy: Whatever that means! Ah, love, the emptiness I sense sometimes just the other side of all these words. All this distinction-making argument, persevering and persevering, while beyond is this everlasting void into which everything will utterly disappear. All these struggles to understand or avoid understanding; all the books and plastic and camel-hair polo coats and cats. No assumptions, no adumbrations, no postulations, no first principles have the slightest reality except what we can give them with still more words. That Russian students' song says it's all of it nonsense compared with eternity. That's no good. It's the wrong scale. Some long views can be too long: they annihilate. We're human beings and we need a human scale.

THORPE: Asa Huntley, how would you like to be remembered?

HUNTLEY: As an anonymous primitive artist whose fragments reflect the barbaric past in the eyes of an humane and transfigured future.

nancy: ... an extinct species is never recreated by its genus.

The
Holy Act
of Water
Contemplation

He saw her staring at the fountain-jet in The Cloisters and he wanted to make love with her in watery places – a raft on the Mississippi, the seventh hole at White Sulphur Springs, the grave of Hart Crane.

They ended up on the coast of Maine, looking at the Atlantic. Here, at least, was plenitude and he felt satisfied. No skimpy fountains. The amorous ocean threw its arms around the rocks, sighed thunderously, swelled itself and spent quantities of love on the sand.

He always felt so sexy at the seaside.

Afterwards she'd kept a picture of him in her mind, standing up to his third rib in that swell of broken water, looking cross. She was swimming – swimming out to sea, it seemed to him. He shouted 'Don't – Go – Any – *Farther*!' at the back of her head. She heard him clearly and swam out much farther than she would have if he hadn't shouted.

She suspected he was afraid of water.

She came in, finally, out of breath, and stood beside him in the surf laughing at the unamused expression on his red face. He watched her furiously. He was a naturally conservative man, particularly when it came to conserving his own life. It would have upset him very badly if she had got into trouble out there and he'd had to decide not to save her. He was in as deep as he wanted to be already. Some of the surges slopping into his arm pits were almost lifting him off his feet.

'Did you know Paul Klee wrote poems?' she asked, while the water rubbed up and down against their bodies.

'Paul Clay?'

'The painter.'

'No.'

'This one, for instance: "Water/Waves on the water/A boat on the waves/On the boat-deck, a woman/On the woman, a man."'

They went up to the motel they'd noticed, the one that was cantilevered over the rocks, and rented the bridal suite because it had a whole wall of plate glass facing out to sea. After dinner they sat in there on the carpet with just one ruby-shaded light burning behind them and watched the waning truculence of Hurricane Bobbie, demoted now to a minor tropical storm. Each time Bobbie whacked the headland the cliffs just tossed up bursts of water in mocking plumes that fell back slowly, like fireworks. That was to show Hurricane Bobbie there wasn't one thing it could do to the coast of Maine that the coast of Maine didn't want it to. The coast of Maine was in a high good mood, they said, sitting on the white carpet (she between his knees). They invented a catalogue of American storms (his knees pressed hard into her sides): tyrones, hurripowers, thurbophoons, cyclonados.

There was no need for any drawing of curtains.

Their bed was as wide as the night was long. One body swam with the other up and down and across it until they drifted dead-man's float upon the buoyant sheets while

Hurricane Bobbie was reduced to spindrift and dispersed on the decamping tide. He slept pressed to her as if she were his life-belt; his arm was a dead weight around her waist.

Down on the beach in the morning they stuck their fingers into some of the liver-coloured sea anemones that were so much, he thought, like prosthetic cunts for rocks. He hadn't ever thought of nature as witty before.

Now that he had committed adultery and she had fornicated it seemed to them that they might as well continue to do it whenever they had the chance. Mostly they had the chance in New York in her apartment, but once chance brought them together in Chicago. In Chicago he'd worn his wedding band. He'd never done that in her company before. In Chicago she'd spent the night alone while he went home to his wife and children on Lake Shore Drive. It had lowered her considerably to see what irreproachable couples occupied the rooms around hers that night in the small, respectable hotel.

That afternoon they had been struggling to love one another on her hotel bed when it had unexpectedly split down the middle and dumped them both on to the floor. They had laughed for a quarter of an hour, much too grateful for such minor comic relief. Then they had shoved the bed together and started over crosswise and it was no better. In the humidity his sweat had dropped down on her like all the tears of the homesick. What she was doing unaccountably depressed her. His prick would not harden properly, no matter what they did to it. There was a moment when he'd thought he'd rather be back at his desk than where he actually was. It was just after she'd looked at the ceiling and said she'd lost contact and couldn't he give her a shout to let her know whether he was in or out. It had reminded him of similar circumstances just a few nights before, when his wife had said, 'Try not to look so much like your mother while you're making love to me.' He'd ducked his face and battened on to her nipple. 'Out,' he'd said in a muffled voice that threatened to break on it. She had shoved another pillow under her head so that she could look down at him. The eyeballs were darting about underneath his closed lids and made the skin bulge in ever-changing places. This had teased her. Why should his eyes dart around like that when he wasn't even looking at anything?

'You don't think I look like my mother, do you? In bed, I mean.'

She said, 'I've never seen your mother – in or out of bed.'

'Haven't I ever showed you her picture?' He'd started to get up to look for his wallet.

'I don't want to see her picture.' She'd pulled him back over her. Some of his chest-hair mated with her eyebrow, begat itching. And nothing more sensational than this had happened for the rest of the day.

Within marriage, though, she'd thought romantically, love wouldn't have all these now-or-never strains. Married lovers could afford to take a day off when it wasn't working. She had this ideal.

He knew that under any circumstances sex could owe a lot more to sheer determination than to lust. If she'd ever asked him he could have told her.

When he was invited to address a conference on The Church and Higher Education in a seedy resort on the New Jersey shore he asked her to go with him. Not actually *with* him, as it turned out.

'You come down on Wednesday on a bus. We can't arrive together.'

She made a hideous face. 'Wait a minute.' He hugged her. She was such a gorgeous, kooky kid. 'What we *can* do and what we *will* do is stay in the same hotel. We'll just have to make it look like a complete coincidence, that's all. There's every chance we'll run into someone who knew one of us back in The Good Old Christian Days. Are you listening to me *at all*?'

She had splayed one hand across her face, pulling down the lower lids, pugging her nose. Thus she regarded him sadly.

'You hang on until four o'clock,' he continued, wishing she would be serious. 'At four you register and I'll arrange to bump into you at the desk. I'll give you a couple of looks – a short one, a longer one – and then I'll say "Oh, excuse me, but aren't you . . . ?"'

What a charade. Anyone who might have known her back in The Good Old Christian Days would certainly be looking out to learn what she was staying in a run-down resort in the middle of an off-season week for anyway.

The third Wednesday in October was unpredictably warm on the Jersey shore. Nevertheless even in the middle of the afternoon whole reaches of the boardwalk were as deserted as the beach. Him and his rotten meetings! To think they could just as well be miles off down the sand together with nothing but gulls to notice them. She leaned her elbows on the broad rail, watching the breakers flatten down to a thin edge and finally to a glassy sheet. After nothing else was left of each submerged impulse, of the wave's huge urge to land, there was wetted sand reflecting shore birds and whenever a bird took off there was always a tidy scallop of water, trimmed with a ruffle of foam, ready to dash up and rub out the scratch-marks in a burst of Stakhanovite housewifery. How domestic it was beside the sea!

A gust of wind crossed the dry ochre sand like a sun-devil cast by a mirror and a brown figure rose up from it and threw a long, vaporous, smoke-blue shadow down towards the sea. Hands braced on hips and thumbs pushed into the waistband of his trunks the figure walked toward the water. He seemed to study the sand as he went. Where it became wet he stopped and twisted his heel in several times. The next thing she knew he was still there, still in the same place, but upside down, balanced on his hands, offering his round heels to the sky. His feet seemed ready to push aside the frail toenail moon. Slowly his straight legs divided and came together, divided and came together. The tiny piece of moon stayed where it was. The late sun brazed his shins, his feet, the whole poised crescent of his body.

Something about him was like the fountain-jet she loved to watch in The Cloisters. He was fixed yet supple like the dancer in that mound of pulsing water, but he did not bob and spin and lash his arms and shake his hair. He did not fling off drops of himself into the air. Calmly his legs divided and came together, the length of his body pivoted slowly from the shoulders under perfect control. For a time he supported his weight on one hand alone. Without ever falling or faltering he performed his rites – for she was sure that he was engaged in something more spiritual than physical. There was no trace of worldly haste or hesitation in a single one of his movements. He knew exactly what he could do and for exactly how long.

This seemed to her wholly admirable.

Near her on the boardwalk a fat man stood on fallen arches under the awning of a salt-water taffy stall. He watched the performance with his hands in his trouser pockets, rattling change. His taut paunch was thrust out in an exaggerated way as if to show that his body could arch too, that it could take the shape of a great drawn bow. He had the arrow for it, too, in case she wanted to know. His brackish glance kept rubbing against her. She ignored it.

Three boys approached the lone handstander on the beach. He flipped over on to his feet and began to instruct them. By then the fat man was staring at her with open lewdness. When she glared at him he dropped his glance to the suitcase at her feet, then looked up again, all insolence. 'You wanna getta man to keep you, babe.'

'Aw babe, I can't even get a man to *take* me on a ten day free trial basis.' She picked up her little suitcase and moved away, careful not to let his jeering cackle push her too fast down the boardwalk.

When she looked at the beach again the performer of handstands had vanished. The three boys were walking away from the sun on long, wavering stalks, articulated in three places. She saw them all suddenly fling up their arms and throw themselves on to the sand. Always too fast, staggering for an instant on bowed arms, knees poking every direction, legs flailing as they toppled sideways, over and over the boys failed to do handstands.

She wished they could get the hang of it. She wished she could get the hang of it herself.

When it was four o'clock she registered at the hotel. She saw him as soon as she went in, loitering near the desk, but she was not supposed to notice – as if it were possible for her ever to see him and not show it! He gave her the two looks while she was waiting for her key. Projecting his voice as if he were trying out for a play he said, 'Aren't you . . . ?' and sounded so silly it made her helpless not to grin at him intimately. She made a face like a senile beaver and squinted at him but immediately was contorted with laughter. 'Oh God, Kenneth!' she groaned 'This is so *crazy*!' And they were right in the middle of those same scribes and Pharisees he'd been trying all afternoon to impress.

Seeing by his aghast expression that everything was already lost she made a general announcement, speaking with the exaggerated clarity of a recorded message. 'WHEN a death has been erroneously posted BY the computer the resurrection OF an ineligible person IS a systems limitation.' Then in her normal, rather angry, voice she continued, 'I *know* he's a married man. What least little difference does that make to *you*? I'm not claiming to be the *official widow*.' She took his arm. 'And now, my love, shall we just twinkle out?'

His speech would be cancelled, of course. Even though he instantly detached himself from her grip by giving a little hop backward, growling 'Get your poaching hands

OFF me!' He couldn't believe what was happening to him.

'Just for a *fraction* of a second I *thought* the woman was a former student of mine and she seized upon my confusion – to *try* to – I don't know by what manner of innuendo – for some sick, sick reason of her own – to make me an *object of scandal.*' He said that he had immediately realized his mistake, that he'd never seen her before in his life, that he would move at once to another hotel though at great inconvenience to himself, and that he hoped that the unhappy woman, who was obviously deranged, would be allowed to *leave town* quietly.

She understood that he was telling her to get back to New York.

'Plays the disclaimer brilliantly, doesn't he,' she remarked to the desk clerk who had been showy about not watching, as if that sort of thing had already happened three or four times since lunch.

She summoned the elevator and carried her own bag to her room on the eleventh floor of the famous hotel. She had paid for it and she intended to stay in it. Who did he think he was, telling her to leave?

The room was remarkably shabby for such a famous hotel. The green paint on the bathroom was goitrous many times over to the point of bursting with the accumulated humidity of countless steamy showers. Whole districts of her carpet were naked of pile. Her window had a slash of gull-shit across it and did not even overlook the ocean but faced west where the town lay spaced out on such level squares of ground that it looked like a toytown on a game board in spite of the prevalence of big frame houses that were much taller than most of the trees. They all had their ears pricked and their eyes turned towards the sea, but what they had before them to contemplate now was the scribble of rusty fire escapes across the brick backs of hotels – a solid row had reared up between the town and the beach after President Coolidge had summered there and caused it to come into fashion.

She stared down into patchy back yards and did not turn away to unpack. Eventually she realized that she was waiting for the management to throw her out.

Why the hell had she just done what she'd done?

'Three things have always been forbidden to women by men: wit, wrath and financial independence. I have all three, if only in primitive forms. I *don't* have *him*. But *he* doesn't have *me*, either.' It was possible that the feeling she had for him was not any kind of love-feeling at all. Certainly it was not patient. It was not kind. It did not endure all things, believe all things, hope all things, did it. The feeling she had for him was greedy and fierce and it had something against him, something against the way he assumed she would always go along with everything he told her to do.

Another thing she'd never had was a moment's guilt over his wife. 'She'll still have everything she'd had before and I'll have so much less.'

A fed-up looking herring gull coasted past her window with its ivy-leaf feet fastidiously tucked up under its ass. It flowed by without a flicker of its wings but its round eye cut her dead and its beak had a disapproving downward curve. That bird looked religious with judgement.

They hadn't been lovers very long and the property settlement was uncomplicated. As soon as she was back in New York she gathered up his letters, his razor, his shaving cream, his photograph, and the café au lait silk pyjamas his mother had given him the first Christmas of his adultery. She was tempted to keep his phallus-shaped bottle of cologne that had the famous initials carved across the top, cunningly stylizing the little mouth of the urethra, but she didn't. She packed everything into a box, together with a pair of his dirty socks and the silver-backed mirror he'd presented to her on her birthday. She mailed the box to Chicago with insufficient postage.

Once or twice when it all struck her as excessively melodramatic she reminded herself that a woman has to do something of this kind at least once in her life unless she has really exceptional luck.

As for him he wrote her a special delivery letter. She marked it RETURN TO SENDER and handed it back to the postman. She ignored the telephone when it rang. A month passed. She still felt widowed. She missed him, not just from her bed but from every humble thing in her life. If she as much as held someone else's hand it made her feel like the most cynical adventuress. Could he ever have felt as cynical as that, those times he'd held *her* hand?

Once she went back to The Cloisters to stare at the furious, hobbled dancer in the fountain-jet. She had only needed to look at it for the first time to see what it really was that others never seemed to notice as they strayed through the garden, glanced indifferently into the stone basin and passed on. That low jet of water was instinct with primeval energy – an abandoned, mad, ecstatic shaman with hunched shoulders and bound ankles, frenziedly shaking its long crystal fringes, lashing its thick plaits. It stood in one spot twisting and thrashing its tethered body, bobbing and bending forwards and backwards, in utter silence at terrific speeds, flinging out drops of itself that hurtled away and were gathered back into itself again. The intensity of its passionate existence always astonished her, and so did the indifference of everyone else to it.

And then it vanished. She had only glanced up at a sparrow and when she looked back her dancer in the fountain was gone. A thrill of pure terror passed through her. How utterly it was gone. A casual custodial hand somewhere, touching a tap–

He continued to send her letters, continued to telephone. She ignored everything. Then, one midnight, exasperated, she answered the telephone. They talked until the sun had left New York and gone to Chicago and left Chicago and gone to Honolulu. They wept and pitied themselves, grew angry and justified themselves, became rational and explained themselves, melted and promised themselves bliss.

'Go away!' she'd said to begin with.
'I shall love you always.'
'You are childish.'
'What is the matter?'
'Do you still love me?'
'My dreams are of you.'
'You pierce my heart!'
'Your sorrows are mine.'
'Our love will be sweet.'
Our love will be sweet as pure water.

The Spoilers

'You have very distinguished face,' the Chinese photographer said to the Professor of Civilization and its Discontents. 'You say yes? I hang your picture in window. Everybody see.'

'Not until I've left the country,' said the professor, a shy man and vain, soon to take up an appointment at a new university in West Africa. Thus at a stroke he satisfied the demands of his shyness, the requirements of his vanity, and the hopes of the Chinese photographer. But within six weeks the professor was back in Bonnersville with his wife and three-year-old son. A local war had broken out in that part of Africa where they had expected to remain for a year and the government had ordered them to leave. Consequently for the length of an idle semester, with every trip into downtown Bonnersville the professor faced himself on College Avenue – exposed, immense, fixed by an action of transitory light, the centrepiece of the photographer's window display. The Chink, as the professor habitually

thought of him, was a lousy photographer, barely compe-
tent for the passport trade and his 'portrait' was little more
than a snapshot enlarged to the dimensions of a theatrical
poster. The professor enjoyed complaining to his colleagues when they commented on his prominence among the
babies, beauty queens, brides and straight-mouthed
Daughters of the American Revolution that at least The
Chink had approached genius in finding, among all the
lights, angles, and possibilities his appearance afforded,
the only combination of them all that cancelled every
trace of distinction. Not a vestige of dignity, forbearance,
intelligence or humour mitigated that jaded and petulant
face. The professor despised The Chink for muffing his job,
but he despised himself no less for the way he felt a secret
satisfaction at the public exhibition of his face.

The Chink's personal interest in the professor's appearance had much to do with his Caucasian hairiness – the
electrified aureole of fox-coloured curls, the dense russet
eyebrows with a broad patch of pure white in the right
one. Under the jut of these eyebrows were small round
poached eyes between meagre lashes as white as a sow's.
The coarse, spurting moustache bent itself around his
dainty mouth and was trimmed, although The Chink did
not know this, after the manner of the embittered Samuel
Clemens. But The Chink's camera took an independent
view and fixed upon the professor's rubescent pout and
drooping irises lifted, as it seemed, in helpless resentment
towards heaven. (The sag-eyed dolorous gaze of a blood-
hound at loose ends in a beet field, commented one of the
professor's students privately to another.) It ignored the
shapely bones of the cheeks and bestowed broad jowls. It
shortened the short, aggressive nose and fused the head to
the torso, leaving the professor looking as neckless as a
neonate. In short, The Chink's camera had so perfectly
caught the professor's characteristic spirit of shabby
dejection and ironic resignation, that the professor's

friends all agreed the photograph was as accurate a portrait of the inner man as anyone could wish for.

But they did not know their inner man very well. Some of them, aware of his history, could appreciate the unintended comment present in the way The Chink surrounded the professor's portrait with nothing but females, so that all about him in the window, fuzzed with inept back-lighting, with flat-planed faces flattened utterly on the camera's lens, were pictures of two or three toddlers in hair-bows, a selection of girls from the Bonnersville High School graduating class, six candidates for University Homecoming Queen, a few engaged young ladies and several chrysalid brides sheathed in the last of their innocence. Arranged around the perimeters were women with church-pillar characters and cast-iron marcels, holders of exalted office in the local chapter of the D A R. Among them at the back of the window was a face emblematic of that ancient and shadowy figure who, according to the professor, had always accompanied him through his dreams – his Tiresias out of Thebes, out of Thebes City, Utah, the professor's home town. It was a one-hundred-year-old woman photographed by The Chink on the day of her centenary, slumped in a wheelchair between a birthday cake and a funerary basket of gladioli. The small black hole of her collapsed mouth was lapped about with concentric wrinkles. Coarse, gratuitous whiskers flourished on her upthrust chin. This void face, cratered and freckled like the moon, stared straight into the black of the camera as no other face dared to do, unable to counterfeit either pleasure or hope, for it had spent all its occasions and exhausted all its faith. After a century of human life it could offer nothing – not wisdom, nor advice, nor comfort. It was the professor's nearest of spiritual kin that had come past everything else to the hollow core of human life where boredom, beyond the horror and the glory, dwells alone.

The professor could have given a name out of his past to

each of the faces around him in The Chink's window. Names of aunts still maiden though long espoused, and great-aunts who had been widows even before he was born; names of wives to the number of two and two identical daughters, twins from the first marriage; names of teachers loved and teachers mocked; names of play-mates, estranged thirty years before by his irritable selfishness; names of girl friends, mistresses, diverse coveted women – some of them his students, some of them wives of his colleagues. Women forced into community under the dominance of his own defeated head. The accurate irony of this store-window display, airless and changeless, pleased the Professor of Civilization and its Discontents and he could say exactly why it pleased him. From his infancy, after his father's ambiguously acciden-tal death, his universe had been a-moon with women and he was its lordly, troublesome sun. But it was not a satisfying cosmos he centred for it was a meaningless one, and the plainer its patterns became to him as he studied them the less hope he held of ever finding any meaning in it. All its creatures were hollow at the core. He himself was hollow at the core, however dense and brilliant his surface. The beauty in the patterns promised pleasure, yielded only pain. He had never been loved and he knew it.

Whelped into the world as his mother was departing it and deserted there after less than a year by his father, who was a coward and a self-murderer – no, perhaps not a self-murderer – the child grew up in a wilderness of female relatives, older and older women who suffered his uncom-fortable presence, his alien sex. They did their best to civilise him by forbidding him movies and the company of little girls. He went to church with them twice on Sundays and to prayer meeting every Wednesday night. All he knew about either one of his parents was what these women would tell him and no one was in any hurry to tell him very much. He spent such time as he could lying cross-wise over his bed, shirtless for the heat, listening to the radio. On Saturday afternoons when there were simulated broadcasts of the baseball games being played in Fenway Park he envied people who lived in Boston where the day was two hours closer to its end than it was in Thebes City. And yet, though he longed for the end of every day he dreaded the coming of night. His dread intensified after he began to produce nocturnal emissions, about which he dared say nothing to his aunts. He took these to be the first signs of his now swiftly approaching death, a kind of cold white bleeding. He was terrified of death. Obsessively he wrote detective stories on ruled notepaper featuring Sergeant 'Red' Grady of Scotland Yard. In Grady's world death did not mark the end of the story but the beginning, signalling a hunt for murderers. That someone should pay with his life for causing the death of the victim was a proposition that interested the young author but the proposition that *fascinated* him concerned the question of motive. The death must have a plausible explanation. The reason for the killing must be hunted down and verified. The right answer must be found, concluding the mystery to the mind's satisfaction, accounting for everything, with none of the loose ends left that stray from real lives.

When he had graduated from the Thebes City High School his aunts sent him to a Mormon college in another part of the state where the ban on smoking, beer, tea, coffee, dancing and cards carried even heavier penalties than those his aunts had imposed, and where every morning the community of scholars gathered in the chapel to 'warship the Lard'. He was soon burning up two packs of Lucky Strike cigarettes every twenty-four hours until his landlady reported him to the Dean of Men and the Dean of Men expelled him. He didn't care. Depression had gone even deeper into him than the fear of dying had, and he knew there weren't ten minutes in his life that he'd care to live over. When someone told him that a few shots of

Ever-Kleer in half a bottle of root beer would either make him passing-out drunk or kill him he sat down on his bed and drank off the Ever-Kleer neat. The last thing he could remember about that night was the trouble it took him to get all the parts of his long, paralyzed body inside the landlady's hall toilet where he had gone to die. It was one thing, he had reasoned, to do damage to himself; quite another to leave a leg out where someone coming along in the dark might get a bad fall. In certain respects his aunts had brought him up rather well.

When he failed to die he was disappointed but not surprised. He had recognized an old pattern turning up in a new place. For the rest of the spring he had worked on a road-gang in eastern Colorado. He continued to smoke two packs of Luckies every twenty-four hours and he added beer-drinking to his sins, and sometimes girls. In the fall he had obtained a scholarship to the state university and proved to be the best student anyone in the Department of Generalities could remember. After two years the Korean War broke out. He enlisted in the air force to escape being drafted into the infantry. Discharged after ten months with compound fractures of the legs after bailing out of his burning plane above Seoul he went back to Colorado, then on to graduate school in California, taking over lectures for his bored professors and breezing through his PhD. His career flourished. He got married. His articles appeared in many journals. His twin daughters were born. And still there were hardly ten minutes in his life he'd care to live over. He felt decently ashamed of this remembering his co-pilot, sitting dead in the cockpit beside him. *It should have been me – but it wasn't.*

He sometimes imagined that he might have made a good monk. He had the capacity for solitude, he thought, if not for piety. But in the year before the divorce, after Alta had taken their daughters and gone back to Thebes City, he realized that even monks are in constant company of sorts by reason of their physical community whereas he in his empty house was utterly alone. He could not endure the deserted rooms and to avoid them he would spend all day on campus, working in his office or in the library when he wasn't in his classroom. He'd written his book that year. Nights he'd established himself in Millie's Tavern, where he quickly became her most famous patron, being as cogently eloquent drunk as sober. Drunk or sober he was the incessant speaker, but drunk he could not let a topic go. He would spin out to infinity ingenious variations upon the few themes that still genuinely interested him: the frigidity of women, the bickering of women, his own moral faultlessness.

In those days he was still only an assistant professor and his classes were very large. He met them in the former concert hall of the old music building, lecturing wittily on human folly while standing on the stage like an actor. The analogy pleased him. Among all the anonymous faces he looked out upon that year the beauty of one distracted him immoderately. When he saw that the co-ed whom he desired wore another man's ring he was determined to have her. They began to meet in his office. One day he reached out and brushed her cheek. '"Was this the face that launched a thousand ships?" That's such a bitter speech, you know. Marlowe's saying that Helen is only an object after all – just a device for extracting men's souls from their bodies. I want you so much, Marilyn Berquist.' There was a silence in which they had looked at one another, utterly absorbed. He thought if he could only get away somewhere he could work it all out. 'Things are manageable when we can reduce them to literature,' he said to her finally. 'I have a Scott Fitzgerald sensibility. If I could just rent a hotel room and have a mouse bite my finger everything would be all right. Give him up, whoever he is, and we will go horribly off into the sunset and there we will be, happy as larks.'

For reasons of her own Marilyn Berquist had agreed to this. Yet after the divorce from Alta was final, after he had a wife in his house again, the professor's expected encounter with happiness still escaped him. He believed that his daughters' now permanent removal from their father's life was filling them with woe. This left a guilt in him that he could not absorb into the pleasure of a new occupation for his mind and body. Too late it came over him that his first marriage had not really been unbearable at all. Alta had been dull but sweet-natured. Marilyn was proving to be both narcissistic and bitchy. Worse, she was sexually unadventurous and before very long seemed completely unresponsive. Alta at least had liked her nooky, liked it often, and would like it still – as he had opportunity to notice each summer when he paid a visit to his daughters in Thebes City. Alta had never been good looking and she was not ageing well. About the time his son was born she'd re-married, which put an end to his child-support payments. He'd never grudged those. Lucille and Loretta were his daughters and he loved them. No. Felt guilty towards them. He would wonder, when he could bear to think about it, how anyone could do to children what he had done to his – for he believed that he had been their whole world. Yet at the time of the divorce the twins simply hadn't counted; he had scarcely even thought about them.

He had formed his permanent concept of ideal feminine beauty early in his life by combining the attributes of his favourite teacher, Miss Spurgeon, with those of admired film stars – for although he wasn't allowed to enter a movie theatre he could circumspectly study the fan magazines displayed in the local drug store. Thus, a beautiful woman would always have on black silk lingerie whatever else she was wearing and in the tumbling of her long blonde hair she would resemble Miss Spurgeon, who taught the fifth grade. But most importantly she would have a nose like Betty Millender's, whose perfect nostrils as she had skated past him on the sidewalk that day of revelation had flared wide. Flared wide – and he had doubled over, a child of ten, thrust through with his first stab of sexual desire. 'Get out of my way, Buddy Cade!' she had cried imperiously as she sped past him with long strokes of her clamorous skates and he had been a nose man ever since. Marilyn had the requisite nose – small, straight, so narrow he wondered how she breathed, and its tip was as shapely as a Moorish arch – but she didn't like nooky. He had more or less understood this before he had married her but he'd believed he could easily change her. He believed that he was to a rare degree the master of sexual technique; that he could excite any woman he chose to until she was in a thrashing frenzy for him; that he had always been able to and that he always would be able to. He was exceptionally easy to fool. A woman who had the patience probably could fool him for the length of a long marriage. But Marilyn didn't want to. Pretence became boring and pretence was abandoned. When the professor complained that after six months Marilyn had turned completely frigid he believed that he had penetrated to some large truths about the nature of women: that for the most part they were simply unequal to him; that they significantly lacked the capacity for sustained passionate response; and that there was simply nothing to be done about it. It could hardly reflect badly upon the professor if he did not seem to please such defective creatures. No man could please them. And as it never occurred to him that he had only exhausted their generosity without approaching the sources of their passion – without even imagining what those sources might be – he remained convinced that at any time he really chose to he could drive any woman into heat. A woman who challenged his assumption was merely bickering, and she was bickering because she was incapable of passionate response and had to resort to some form of substitute gratification for her stunted instincts.

The professor understood all these things very clearly. His now large academic reputation rested principally upon the book he had written about Susan B. Anthony during the year of his divorce. He was supposed, on the evidence of that work, to possess unusual insight into the enigmatic nature of those few women who had found secure places in anyone's history of civilization. Male assistant professors and graduate students began to seek him out for his knowledge of the feminine soul. He answered them if he deemed their queries worthy of it by confidently referring to dysmenorrhea, amenorrhea, scanty or irregular menses and the absence of the penis in the female. There was nothing deficient in civilization worth accounting for, it seemed to him, that could not be explained by reference to female reproductive physiology: its pathology and specific deficiencies.

Now that he was five years into his second marriage the professor more and more frequently recalled his favourite West African proverb: the eye seeks its cinder. Now he believed he saw his situation clearly at last, and seeing it, felt unwilling ever again to try to force the patterns to yield him pleasure. He was convinced now that from the moment of his conception he had been unjustly wronged and that he suffered more intensely than other men the sharp pain of unremitting consciousness. He was confirmed in feeling that nothing that happened to him could ever really be his fault. He complained of his wives that they had both continually bickered with him, that they cared more for what others thought of them than for what he thought, that the feelings of strangers received more consideration from them than his own feelings ever did, that the chronic domestic tensions which troubled both his marriages stemmed directly from the bickering of the women, that their bickering had spoiled the marriages, that nothing had been his fault. The women who attracted him were all alike. They had to be, for does the eye not seek its cinder? At bottom it was that simple and that unlucky and nothing about it was his fault. He couldn't help it if women bickered. A third wife, and a fourth, would bicker too. Unable to see that he created bickering women out of his insatiable need for them, he insisted instead that it was in the very nature of women to bicker, malignantly to attack his most vulnerable tissues.

We ought to keep our desires secret – since once they are known they can be half granted. This thought made him strangely happy.

The professor had a lust for gossiping. He believed that his colleagues at Bonnersville envied him his style in gossiping, that his style was best when subtly malicious. He was especially fond of gossip about the chairman of the Sociology Department whose popularizing books on social anthropology had become best-sellers. Perry was a household name. Industrialists and politicians courted him, quoted him. The professor liked to tell people that Perry was in the habit of giving his little daughter a cigarillo and asking her to smoke it while he watched. 'Perry enjoys the aesthetics of this. Bizarre, you see. Like an angel smoking a churchwarden. That's a kind of pipe, in case you don't know. Have I told you yet about the time Perry introduced me to Adams Fairchild in the john at the Harvard Club? Fairchild might be the governor of New York but he pisses like other men and that is what he was doing when Perry introduced us. He was having a piss and old Perry, our renowned chairman and household name went up to him – I was with Perry, you see – old Perry went right up to him and said "Adams, I want you to shake hands with a brilliant young man from Utah." Fairchild had his dong in his hands, of course. I'll say this much for him, he is prodigiously equipped – he had both hands around his dong, so he simple threw Perry a filthy look and me a sort of helpless smile. Of course old Perry didn't notice. Old Perry's an ass. There's a rude verse everyone in the field knows by now: Consider Perry/Old clothes on a peg/With nothing on his mind/And nothing down his leg.' The professor accepted the applause of his audiences modestly enough after such recitals but he also accepted the silent censure that he knew came not from envy but from blame. The shame and the elation he felt then pleased him. They gave him an almost sexual pleasure.

From adolescence onwards he had believed with Charles Williams that the ideal state for man was 'not to be and never to have been'. And now because of that photograph he felt as removed from this ideal state as he had ever felt in his life, immense in The Chink's window, completely surrounded by women, idled for a semester, utterly bored, The Distinguished Professor of Civilization and its Discontents, Doctor Graydon Cade, cowardly adulterer, reaper of whirlwinds.

* * *

The depot where Kathleen Post had waited for the bus out of Bonnersville early on a Saturday morning in January was just opposite the Chinese photographer's shop and as she stood in line to board her coach she'd glanced over at it. Professor Cade's portrait had been taken out of the window at last and Kathleen missed it. As long as it had been there, because she loved Graydon Cade, she had wanted it taken down. Now and for the same reason she wanted it put back – her own modest portrait was on display now that she'd won a state-wide piano competition. It seemed as if they were never meant to be together, not even in The Chink's shop window.

Never meant to be together. Surely that was why, all day, the planes had been late. One by one, two hours – three hours – four hours behind schedule, from the circling stack invisible in the storm clouds, the planes had come in at last. All but Cade's. His flight had been delayed in leaving San Francisco, stacked for an hour over O'Hare, diverted to Toledo after dark. It had re-fuelled, returned to O'Hare, and circled for another hour, finally getting permission to land in the near-blizzard. Kathleen had been waiting in the terminal since noon. Cade's first glimpse of her, as he came along the docking ramp, disappointed him. She looked strained, closer to the age he knew she was. She had on a coat he had not seen before and its fluffy fur collar disarranged the ends of her hair. She had been rained on, she explained, waiting to change buses. In the hotel he sent the aged and reluctant bellhop down the hall for a bucket of ice while he unpacked the bourbon. Later they would have dinner, but his first hunger was for Kathleen. Under her new coat was a matching kelly green dress. He told her it was pretty and then he took it off her to enjoy the familiar black lace, silk, and flesh beneath. Her disordered hair looked all right now, proper to intimacy. It was going to be okay. Without her clothes she was still the finest looking white woman he had ever seen and he told her so, outright. She could just about believe him.

'How was San Luis?' she called from the bathroom where she was watering her tumbler of whisky.

'It was all right.' His voice held its usual plaintive note. Life was imperfect. He resigned himself. 'It was okay. Not great, but it was okay.'

She brought the tumbler to the bed and sat down beside him where he lay naked except for the elastic bandages around his legs. He was smoking a cigarette. 'Have you had any adventures since the day before yesterday?' he asked.

'No. Have you?'

'No.'

'No adventures in California?'

'Looking over a sociology department is not the stuff of adventure.'

'I'm not sure. It could be.'

'They *did* give me a very nice party last night and I charmed the pants off them. They offered me a lot of money.'

'Are you going to go then?'

'No.'

He was aware again, as he had been aware earlier on the

plane, as indeed he had known even before leaving Bonnersville, that 'the California thing' was a digression. A means of getting out of Bonnersville to this hotel in Chicago with all his expenses paid. He always felt restless in Bonnersville, of course; always glad of a semester's leave, a sabbatical year. But he was pretty contented with his university. The town was too small, that was all. Sometimes he thought how good it would be to drive with Kathleen into the country somewhere, across state lines. It wouldn't be good. It never was, never had been good. Before. With any of the others. They were all the same. Routine took the glamour out of it. He told her he'd had another dream. 'You and I were in the public library. NO SMOKING signs were everywhere you looked. I was smoking furiously, and frowning and holding my cigarette this way, you see, between my thumb and my index finger. Dragging on it so hard I was nearly biting the tip off. We were looking up the meaning of "lust" in all the dictionaries. A crowd of people – representing society, you see – stood around us, at a respectful distance, muttering disapproval. It could easily have turned ugly. It's very plain that the cigarettes were a substitute gratification. What was interesting about this dream was the way the investigation into lust went almost untampered with by my internal censor. By God that pleased me!'

So what he had wanted then was simply a weekend away with Kathleen and he had been wanting it for months. Now he had it – the freedom of Chicago. This was going to be the great night of his life. He stubbed out his cigarette and put down his tumbler. 'Darling.' He drew her across him and gave her a long kiss while her hand curled around his penis. It leaped when she touched it. His tongue flickered at her nostrils. He gathered up her hair and sifted it through his fingers. 'So fine – like "gold to airy thinnessse beat."' He played at putting it all into a pile on the crown of her head and told her how handsome it looked that way, and then he drew it all back at the nape and said that

looked fine too. He meditated on the perfect straightness
and hardness of her nose and gave her an Eskimo kiss. He
wondered briefly what she was thinking about. She
answered him with her hand. 'Oh darling, darling,
darling.' He rolled on to her, Amor arrayed. Willing as she
was, though, it was too soon for her. Impatiently probing
her dry, resisting flesh he blunted himself. 'I can't do it
right now,' he whispered. 'But that's okay. Later on, I'll
fuck you till your ears fly off.' He smiled across her
shoulder. 'I don't *love* you, you understand,' he said. The
bourbon was taking hold now. Dr Frank Grady could say
things that Professor Graydon Cade could not say. It had
been Dr Frank Grady who had declared upon first meeting
the gentle Japanese bride of a colleague in Bonnersville
that Truman had been absolutely right to drop the bomb
on Hiroshima. Then he'd repeated a slogan from his hoard
of childhood memories about the war. 'Every time you buy
a bond /You slap a Jap across the pond.' 'Saunders should
have kicked me all the way down the street for saying a
thing like that,' said Cade. 'But he didn't. He didn't do
anything at all. Well, shall we get ready for dinner?'

It had only been because he was bored and because she
had a perfect nose that Graydon Cade had paid any
attention at all to Kathleen Post. That was the simple
truth. He had wanted to get his rocks off. He was perfectly
frank about it. 'Don't misunderstand me. What my
attitude comes down to can be put this way: I'll take what
I want from your life, but don't you *ever* interfere in mine.'
Kathleen had accepted his terms, choosing to believe
Cade's candour was an instrument of deception by which
he hoped to mislead her concerning his true worth, for she
believed his worth was immense and a burden to him.

'I'm a superb liar,' he had assured her. 'But I don't lie to
you.'

'You're lying to me when you tell me you never lie to
me.'

His expression had simulated astonishment mixed with genuine delight. 'That's *very* good!'

She'd smiled slightly.

'And don't give me one of your snarky smiles.'

'That's not a snarky smile. That's an archaic smile. The smile of an archaic snark.'

Kathleen dealt with the imperfections in people she loved by assigning them mythical natures and desirable attributes and then behaving towards them as though they actually possessed those qualities. She invented her lovers and then loved her inventions. Sometimes her own needs overwhelmed her and her fragile strategy failed, but as long as she could think mostly of the other person and act for his good her tactic seemed to work. Hadn't she accepted the terms of Franklin Gardiner Bridger's celibacy and kept them faithfully for almost eight years? And so, when Graydon Cade had said to her after many clandestine visits to her flat, 'Kathleen, I love you and nothing can ever come of it. I love you, and that's absurd,' she had decided to believe that illicit love was the highest form of love because it was the most costly, the loneliest.

Women want love and they settle for sex.

Kathleen had never wanted to have a history of lovers. She had wanted to live for one man all her life. Consequently before every new affair now she passed through a crisis of intention. She would have no more of men. She had already passed through this crisis several months earlier with Graydon. It had been resolved for her as soon as she saw that his motives were all too obviously selfish. They were so selfish they *had* to be the mask that his real motives wore. She would not believe that his hierarchy of concerns could possibly be what he insisted it was. For example, he had said that it was supremely important to him how a woman looked. She must look young and be beautiful. 'You could have the loveliest soul in Blakemore

County but I would never know it if your nose weren't
fetching. And it's very easy to disgust me. I loathe red eyes,
for instance. Red eyes disgust me. Never let me see you
with red eyes. You do turn me on, darling, but you can
turn me off too. Just show up some day with red eyes.' He
had continually stressed the impermanence of the affair,
pointing out that a double life was precarious for him and
that should he ever have to make a choice it would not be
in her favour. His marriage was not a happy one, but for
the sake of his new little son he would not rock the boat.
He *would* not.

Nobility was the attribute Kathleen invented for Cade.
She knew a noble nature lay at the bottom of him and she
believed she had the power in her to salvage it. By insisting
upon his essential fineness she would be able to redeem
him (though she herself would not have said redeem). She
believed that she was a generous woman. It had always
been, for her, the most moving moment in their loving
when, with breath calm again and the blood-storm
ebbing, he would turn to her and thank her. His simple
gratitude for his pleasure was the whole of her own
pleasure. It affirmed her estimation of his character. He
was a noble and misunderstood man.

The more difficult he made it for her to accept him as
her lover the more she flew to his defence. She knew that
Graydon Cade's vaunted cuntsmanship was his delusion,
that in fact he was a clumsy and unimaginative lover. It
was his noble potential and his modesty in masking it that
fascinated Kathleen and melted her heart, just as Bridger
had melted her heart years before with his unfulfilled
potential for purely human happiness. Franklin Gardiner
Bridger, eminent scholar and president of The Christian
Institution, her first serious love and a bachelor to his
death, had made his bountiful soul balm for the gross
itching of the flesh, so that more than anything else
Kathleen had longed to corrupt him into that becoming
humanhood for which he seemed to her to be so richly

fitted. Bridger had never taken a woman in his life and he did not take Kathleen, even though once or twice in the beginning he had seemed to approach her as if he might. Desire for women and fear of them were mixed equally in him, giving Kathleen her sustaining faith that some day she would be the agent through which he would free himself from his sense of the sin in human sexuality, the death there.

Graydon Cade had given up his plan for a bit of cocktail-hour nooky with Kathleen. He was sitting in the bathtub among pubic hairs from some previous guest, staring gloomily between Kathleen's thighs and wishing he had met *her* seven years ago instead of Marilyn.

'Would you have liked me then, do you think?'

'We'll never know that,' she replied, 'unless we can find someone who's able to foretell the past.' She added after a moment's thought that probably she *wouldn't* have liked him then because she would still have been absorbed in Franklin.

'What am I going to do about you?' Now he knew what it was that he hated – it was the way she doled herself out to the needy. She seemed to think that if she had some love going spare and saw someone who needed it then she had to give it to him. That kept her all bountiful and superior, didn't it. That's what he hated about her. *She* didn't need anyone. And taking love from her he'd grown fond of her, which he had never meant to do. 'He who travels fastest travels alone,' he said at the conclusion of these reflections.

'Where are you going, then?' Her long naked back glimmered.

'I knew you'd ask that. The night before I flew out to San Francisco I had a dream. You and I were in Dallas, in a hotel room. A former student of mine, one Harvey Erlich, drat him, had just been appointed president of the university at Bonnersville. I don't know what he was doing in Dallas. He came up to the room to see me. Under the circumstances it seemed advisable to stow you in the bathroom. Erlich had always been a bore but he outdid himself on this occasion. I was afraid he'd ask to use the toilet before he left – if he was ever going to leave. I hoped you'd have the presence of mind to step behind the shower curtain if he did. When he finally left without a piss I found you in the bathroom absolutely naked with what I took at first to be a comb in your hand. It was in fact a knife. You said "if I can't have you no one will" and came towards me with the blade presented. I started awake with a gasp that woke Marilyn. It was clear to me that I had been about to breath my last.'

'What a horrible dream!' said Kathleen, enjoying it, very pleased.

'Have you ever dreamed about me?'

'Not really. I did dream once that I couldn't find your office. I was supposed to meet you there. I was wandering all over the Generalities Building. There weren't any rooms in it – only long, narrow, inclined planes. But of course that's not the same as dreaming about *you*.'

'How did you feel when you couldn't find me?'

'Oh, very disappointed.'

'You see, what's important about a dream is how the dreamer feels about what happens in it. You were searching for me and that's nice. You wanted to find me. That's what's important.'

Graydon Cade lay back in the tub, the better to watch Kathleen as she stood opposite him, making up her face at the mirror. He had always loved to watch women putting on make-up. The contorted features excited him – the drawn noses, the twisted mouths. '"It is a prick, it is a sting, It is a pretty, pretty thing"' he quoted mockingly and fingered the crown of his penis. *She should have been ready for me, though. She says she loves me. Then why can't she let me in.* He felt the same kind of disappointment he had experienced earlier at the airport when he had expected so much and received so little. That morning

– how long ago it seemed – in his California hotel he had only to think of Kathleen's nose to produce immediate tumescence; now in the same room with it he couldn't lift a wiggle. In the plane he had lubricated at the thought of her waiting for him when he landed, the loveliest woman in the Middle West, and how she would run up to him through the staring crowds to kiss him and show the envious travellers how the loveliest woman in the Middle West felt about *him*. When that meeting finally took place no one had stopped to watch and nothing at all had dribbled down his leg.

For dinner Cade took Kathleen to Casa Italiana, an overrated restaurant in the Loop that he naively supposed would be both good and inexpensive. He ordered drinks before they opened the menu. Predictably, she thought, he recommended the ravioli. She did not want ravioli. She wanted prosciutto and melon, fettucine verde, ossobucco, peaches in syrup, coffee with grappa. She'd had nothing to eat all day, first for the excitement of getting to the airport, later the tension of waiting there so long. When the waiter returned Cade ordered ravioli for them both.

'With sauce or *al forno?*' asked the waiter. Cade was not aware the choice existed.

'*Al forno,*' said Kathleen quickly, her vowels pure and stressed. The waiter flashed her a smile.

'Sauce,' said Cade.

The waiter brought antipasto and more drinks. Cade asked him for the wine list. The waiter showed him where it was printed on the menu. Cade studied it irritably. 'Is that everything you have?'

'Yes, sir,'

Cade pointed to one of the wines. 'Is this good?'

'Yes, sir. That's very nice.'

'Bring us a bottle of that, then.'

Moving off the waiter glanced at Kathleen. She couldn't help returning a small conspiratorial smile.

Casa Italiana had several dining rooms and two bars.

The room where Graydon and Kathleen were seated had a close, well-like atmosphere despite the shrimp-pink plaster walls. The putti painted on the ceiling seemed much too far from the flowers in the carpet. Kathleen was dizzy after her drinks. Cade appraised each woman in the room and then with satisfaction reported to Kathleen that she was without any doubt the finest looking wench present.

'Remember when I took you out to lunch last month? That was to make sure you knew how to use a fork before I brought you here.' Kathleen laughed, not knowing how else to respond. 'No. I mean that seriously. Lots of people just don't know. Alta used to hold her fork this way.' Cade closed his fist around the shaft of his fork. 'She'd just shovel her food in. That's how everyone in Thebes City ate. *You're* very delicate about it, though, aren't you. You curl your little pinkie all up and then stick it right out there just like a princess.'

Kathleen's demeanour had from the beginning, both fascinated Cade and put him off. Before he knew anything about her he had assumed her airs and graces came to her honestly. Then she'd told him her father was a steamfitter. He understood her to be joking. Only after she'd convinced him it was the truth did he find it possible to tell her *his* father had been a self-murderer. Possibly.

When the ravioli came Cade compared the two dishes and petulantly inquired why Kathleen's food was different from his.

'It isn't different. I ordered *al forno.* You ordered sauce. It's all ravioli underneath.'

Cade didn't understand this, but he let it go. Had he been sober, or lacking for a particular complaint he would have pursued that mysterious distinction relentlessly, but he was about to broach a matter which, now that he was somewhat drunk, excited him to the exclusion of everything else: the death of Franklin Gardiner Bridger and the manner in which Kathleen had learned of it. 'Frankie is dead,' he began. 'You pick up your newspaper one morning and you read the headline – no, it wouldn't be quite headline stuff way out here – you see it, let us say, on page two. Perhaps even page three. And that is how you learn that Frankie is dead. For there is no one to tell you personally, no one to send you a telegram saying that the love of your life is no more. That task falls to nobody in Frankie's world because in that world of big, important, high-powered people you are nobody. So you go back east all by yourself to the funeral and you do not cry. You had been faithful to him for eight long years and you are really his widow, you see. You are really his unacknowledged widow – for, am I not right, he was unmarried and you had loved him faithfully for the last eight years of his life –'

Kathleen listened to this in appalled silence. When tears began dripping into her lap she stood up.

'You're crying for him now, though, aren't you. Yes. You'd better go fix yourself up. Your eyes are getting red.' Cade's mouth hung slack over the rim of his wine glass, showing the small brown teeth set deep inside. His hound's eyes fixed her in a stare that followed her out of the room. She didn't know where she was and blundered into one of the bars. Where for the love of God was the ladies' lounge? The barman directed her down some stairs.

Franklin Gardiner Bridger had been The Event of Kathleen's life. The first human being she had known towards whom she wanted to be openly affectionate and felt able to be without fear of rebuff. But not for long. Before she had known him a year his antique mother had died. After that, to Kathleen's bewilderment, Bridger had closed himself to her, made it seem almost a breach of etiquette for her to say she loved him. He recoiled from the words. She felt this even when she spoke them over a telephone or wrote them in a letter. Then whenever they met, never often and never for long, he had started saying things that made her shiver. 'Why do you touch me – are you trying to annoy me?' And one night at dinner, 'Why

must you stare at me like that. I wish you wouldn't stare.'
Then later, 'I've never told you that I loved you, have I.
I have never let myself love you.' That, of course, was true.
He never had said he loved her; he had simply behaved
towards her as though he loved her and that was what she
believed in – his behaviour. He was gentle and courteous
and circumspect. She understood he didn't want to make
a fool of himself. Sometimes she wanted to say to him that
the cruellest thing of all was to be saved for sentimental
reasons, but she couldn't say it. She knew, but she could
not help it, that nothing is more embarrassing to a man
than the faithfulness of a woman he no longer wants. The
faithfulness of the one only makes both appear ridiculous,
although somehow it makes the ridiculous woman seem
touching as well, while the man looks merely cynical. It
was inconceivable to Kathleen that Bridger should ever be
anywhere but at the centre of her life, whatever place she
had in his, and it was therefore inconceivable that anyone
else should ever supplant him there. She accepted the shift
in their relationship stoically. He had taught her that one
must always be thoroughly discriminating in one's choice
of things to feel sad about and that to be very sad, or sad
for very long, was the sign of a weak character. It almost
seemed to her sometimes that his ideal for human
existence had been never to acknowledge the existence of
anything human.

Franklin Bridger, who was so very much older than
Kathleen, began to feel more and more like a child again
whenever he was with her after his mother's death. He had
been his mother's only child and she had comforted him
with silent affection. There had been no overt sentimentality in Bridger's relationship with his mother while she
was alive, which encouraged him to believe there had
been no sentimentality in it at all. They had touched each
other lightly, made jokes of everything they could.
'Franklin will marry you,' his mother had told Kathleen

once. 'He'll make a wonderful husband. Not selfish, like most men.'

The reasons Franklin gave Kathleen for not ever wanting a sexual relationship with her were, as he saw it, reasons of religious conviction, having to do with reverence for God and respect for His creation, her body. Thus shielded he could approach dread oedipal matters with radical innocence, treating them as intellectual jokes, because the seriousness of life lay elsewhere. 'You see,' he told Kathleen, his eyes twinkling at her solemn ones, 'the real reason I won't let myself sleep with you is that I'd feel as though I were in bed with my mother, isn't that right?' He chuckled, unembarrassed. But when he went on to state once more what he believed was his *real* reason his tone was as solemn as Kathleen's face. 'You see, if bone and blood and all the urges in them can be directed upward, channelled toward a higher goal than the gratification of the body, why, I think that's fine. Now you'd argue, wouldn't you, that this is conventional. Well, the word "conventional" means "a coming together", doesn't it. And if enough comes together, why, that's integrity. Integrity is the wholeness a person achieves by going through thick and thin with another person. Anything else is just romanticism. That's not to say it's no good, but it isn't love and can't be called love. It's in that sense, I think, that I'm conventional. And you are too. You really are.'

Hearing this, Kathleen's flesh had prickled with admiration and shame. She could never live up to him. He was pure Olympian.

'When I die,' he'd gone on after a silence, 'there won't be anyone to tell. There's no family left, now my mother is gone. There isn't a living soul they can tell.'

What about me, she'd wanted to say. I'm a living soul. They can tell me.

Sitting alone at their table with another drink Graydon Cade cherished the deeply satisfying pang that came from his certain knowledge that no one would ever mourn for him the way Kathleen mourned for Frankie, that son of a bitch. She was away a very long time. Perhaps she'd gone back to the hotel. If so, she had gone without her coat which was still over the back of her chair. That god-damned hovering waiter was keeping his eye on Cade. *He* was on Kathleen's side, of course, the frigging, cocksucking wop. No gentlemen would ever make a lady cry. Well, Graydon thought, I've never claimed to be a gentleman. He caught the waiter's eye in a concentrated stare and the waiter moved off leaving Cade irritably aware of the snub-nosed youthfulness of his own face. Even in maturity, when the experienced flesh should draw the features of a face into their most harmonious relationship, achieving the character towards which they have been tending for half a lifetime, faces like Cade's don't, but pass straight from spurious youth into ruin. Cade was aware of the fleshy welts inside his bitten cheeks, the bitten fingernails each with a thin line of black where the flesh swelled over the horn, the leg livid, cold with scars, and a twenty-one-year-old-airman dead in the cockpit beside him.

What if Kathleen really had gone back to the hotel and left him to sit here like a fool? He didn't want to go back to the hotel. He wanted to go to London House for jazz and a lot more bourbon. Oh for Christ's sake, were they in Chicago on Saturday night for nothing? Kathleen appeared at the dining room door at last, looking distressed and hardly more attractive than when she had left. Once again, examining her as if she were a stranger, he decided he didn't like her hair. Or that ridiculous muff of black fur that dangled from her wrist. Or that summer-silk print she was wearing in the midst of winter. Why would she wear a dress like that anyway? Because she had no taste. That's why. No taste. After all, he concluded with satisfaction, her beauty had only been potential. It had not been realized and now it never would be. She was getting too old. And she can't drink. Look at her. Stumbling on the carpet. Her eyes swelling up. She can't drink. She wouldn't have looked like this in public with *him,* her Great Man, Frankie her frigging Olympian. He'd had her when she was at her best, when she might really have been beautiful. If he'd never made anything of that, so much the worse for him. *That bastard. I hate his guts. If I ever see him in the next world I'll kick him in the balls.*

Kathleen sat down without looking at Cade and disengaged her muff. They sat in silence, he smoking, she picking at her cold ravioli. The waiter came back, the ubiquitous dago, to see whether they wanted anything else. Cade ordered another drink for himself. *He doesn't want to get me one, does he.*

Cade watched the waiter pugnaciously. *He thinks I've had enough, the cocksucking wop.* The waiter turned to Kathleen. Nothing more? Coffee? She shook her head, unable to look up from her plate. The corners of her mouth turned down as she tried to smile. 'A dish of spumomi?' the waiter urged. She loathed the suggestion, accepted it to get rid of the waiter whose unspoken sympathy oppressed her. 'Thank you. That would be very nice.' To her surprise her voice was firm and controlled. How had she done it? And if she could do that why couldn't she stop the fountains of her eyes?

The waiter cleared the table leaving nothing for Kathleen to do with her hands. She took out a cigarette. Cade ignored her search for a match. The waiter darted in with a flourish and presented fire. 'Can't you just leave us alone for five minutes?' Cade said in a voice that was calm with hatred. Kathleen smoked her cigarette in silence. 'I thought you'd gone off to the hotel.'

'Not without my coat.'

He watched her for a moment, full of revulsion. 'Well, you tuned right up, didn't you. You tuned right up for Frankie.'

In the cab Graydon proposed London House. Kathleen preferred the hotel. She was, to herself, like a marsh, a swamp, a useless sopping remnant of earth almost gone back to water. In the hotel she undressed immediately, changing into the expensive black gown she'd bought with such joy for this night, especially to delight Graydon. Her face in the mirror appalled her. How could a few tears wreak such ruin? She left the bathroom and crossed to the bed where Graydon was lying in his shorts and elastic bandages, a tumbler of bourbon beside him, one light burning in the corner behind an armchair. She did not want to look at him or to have him look at her. She lay down on her back with her arm across her eyes.

'You should give up everything for me,' Graydon said.

'What makes you think I have a single solitary thing to give up?'

'I could easily drive my car into the river some day. Easily.' He'd already told her that he only kept on living because he didn't know of any dignified way to stop, that all he dreaded about death was the indignity of it.

'Aren't you going to have a drink?'

'No. I don't want anything.'

'All right,' he said cheerfully. 'I'll drink alone. I'm not sleepy.' He was satisfied. She was like all the others – wilful, self-centred, meanly impenetrable. The notion that she might truly be different from the others had never altogether pleased him anyway, for if she had been truly different he should have been tormented by the existence of a living ideal inaccessible beside him, and all that he had habitually come to accept in his second marriage might have become intolerable.

Marriage is a rotten institution. He often said so. A woman must be beautiful, intelligent, talented – and absolutely adoring. But he very well recognized that if the creature possessed the first three of these attributes it was all but impossible she could possess the fourth with reference to anyone except herself. *Marriage is a rotten institution.*

This woman beside him, lying with her back to him,

with her pillow in her arms, was adoring – but not of him. 'The undeserving bastard. If I ever meet Frankie in the next world I'm going to kick him in the balls. That's assuming he has any. Why won't you drink with me?' Kathleen kept silent – too intelligent to imagine argument or answer would have any point. The dead are past defending and the living too sad to rebuke. Now her tears were for herself alone. She deserved better men than these she had known. Better than Bridger who, in his selfish purity, had chained her outside his door and left her there starving for eight years. Better than Graydon, who had warned her not to mistake his candour for honour. Once she had called him tender, gentle and considerate. Now he gloried to show her how mistaken she had been.

Cade was feeling well-satisfied. Again he had proved his power over women. He could destroy all their beauty and desire. He could turn them into so much salt water. He could lay them in ruins and look at them with loathing. What brackish things were these? He could turn them on and turn them off. He was the master of revels and the king of pleasure; the prince of passion and the prince of pain. Frank Cardinal Grady, Archbishop of Puritania. The Honourable Sir Graydon Cade, Lord of the Lyre and Lord of the Light's Edge.

'I think I turn you on sexually,' he said. 'I don't think Frankie was a very good lay. I think he was a decent diddler. Have I ever told you, when we first began to fuck you did something I hated. You used to make your hand into a fist and hold it over your cunt. That was Frankie's doing, wasn't it.' She did not answer. 'Oh all right. Go to sleep ... You can't drink, you know. Two drinks and you're finished. Your eyes swell shut. You're disgusting.' He stared at the wall beyond the foot of the bed, sipping until his glass was empty. 'You're like all the others. You want to cut off my balls, don't you. You hate my guts, don't you ... I want another drink. Why won't you drink with me? ... Oh all right, I don't care. That's okay. You sleep. You lie there and hug your little pillow. It's the little baby Frankie wouldn't give you, isn't it. That's okay.' He went into the bathroom. Kathleen could hear him making a fresh drink. Never mind what he said. The pillow received the unsummoned tears after the flooded gutters of her eyes could not contain them. It was more comfort to her than the living or the dead. She could hear Graydon pissing, a scanty trickle nothing like the rich, full-spated pissing of women. He came back to the bed. She hoped he might reach out now and touch her. It could still be good between them, in the dark where he could not see her eyes.

'I can't sleep,' he complained. She heard a match scrape and pop into flame. 'I'm not sleepy ... You can't fuck, either. You're frigid, you know. Old frigid Kathleen. Mrs Kinney – you remember Mrs Kinney, she wrote me the best dissertation on Durkheim any student of mine ever wrote – Mrs Kinney was up one wall and down the other. Not like you. Mrs Kinney was in my office on Monday, you know. You don't know. She was in my office. She told me I was going to go to heaven ... Old frigid Kathy. God, I hate your name ... I'm Dr Frank Grady and I'm drunk. I drink, you know. Do you know why I *really* hate Frankie, that son of a bitch? I hate him because he had you when you were young. He had you when you really were beautiful, because you're not any more, you know. You weren't very pretty tonight. When you met me at the plane and ran up to kiss me you weren't very pretty. Your hair didn't look very nice. And now your eyes are swollen shut from just a little bit of night life. Two little drinks. And you have an old-looking, saggy belly. Did you know that? You have a regular little pot there ... While you were in the ladies' room weeping over Frankie I decided to call you up. The phone went "blllpp, blllpp," and in your old-lady voice which I am now going to imitate, you said "Hellloooo?" and I said "Kathleen?" God, I hate your name. Why isn't your name Frieda or Agnes or Vagette? I loathe your name.

So – hokey Irish and pretentious. It's so . . . Kathleen, why don't you love me more than you *ever* loved Frankie? I love you. No, I don't really. That's not true. Oh, Kathleen – God, I hate your name – what am I going to do? I think I've come to the end of my endurance. Why can't you orbit in my rainbow? You despise me, don't you . . . You hung up on me. The phone went "blllpp, blllpp" and you hung up on me . . . I can't sleep. Two, four, six, eight. Kathy's going to menstruate . . . Why don't you love me more than anyone? I'm so hung up on you . . . I fucked Marilyn on the morning I left. Not to her satisfaction. But it was all right. She took the little boy to nursery school and when she came back I fucked her. Old frigid Marilyn. It wasn't very good, but it was all right. It was okay. Have you prayed tonight for Frankie? I imagine that every night before you get into bed you kneel down and say: "God grant him peace." That's what I imagine. If I got killed on the highway would you do that for me? I just want somebody to be down in the abyss, looking up at me and crying out my name over and over with adoration. "Absalom, Absalom." And I would toss a crumb down to you, or a hyena's ear. Why did I say a hyena's ear? That's a strange choice of parts. There are more horrible parts. I could have said a hyena's anus. Why did I say a hyena's ear? But that's okay. I'm hollow at the core and I don't like to think about it . . . I don't want to think about that. My little son is lying at home asleep this very minute, unaware of what his father is doing. He wouldn't like to know. He wouldn't like it. . . . If I could get custody of the little boy, would you . . . would you . . . I can't sleep, Kathy. Look at you, passed out from two little drinks. You can't drink. And your father was a steamfitter. That won't do, you know. You'd have to be the banker's daughter.' Graydon turned to Kathleen, lifting himself on to his elbow, trying to see her face. 'I can't stand to have anyone else touch you and that's very hard to say but that's what it is, you see. It's very hard to say. And I can't stand to be rejected by a woman.'

Kathleen abandoned her pillow and put her face to his. In a voice that was dim and choked she said, 'I love you, Graydon. I don't love Franklin any more. I love *you.*' And it was a lie but it satisfied him, and he fell asleep.

The heat in the room was hellish. Kathleen's gown burned her like cloth of fire. She felt heavy as a lake. Flesh floats in water. *I was never flesh.* The force of her pulse seemed to bulge out the bones of her skull. She felt too sick now to travel. Perhaps Graydon could just leave her here until she felt well again. '*Oh, when shall I be well again?*' *What was that, some poem.* She had a dirty feeling in the pit of her stomach but whether it was from hunger or sickness she could not tell.

When the curtains at the window began to collect grey light in their folds she was still awake. For a long time she watched Graydon, lying as he had fallen asleep, on his back, his goatish muzzle open, his skin without tone or colour, the flesh around his eyes only a darker shade of grey than the flesh of his face. It could be a corpse she was looking at. It would be a corpse soon enough. He was killing himself. His flesh was smoked through and through. It gave off a sweet scent. And the hidden organs of his body, secretly poisoned, already caused him insomnia and sour stomach, prostatitis and haemorrhoids. But it would be the smoke, she decided, working in his gills. A spot on the X-ray some day, a biopsy, an operation, an obituary. At least she wouldn't have to watch the dying.

Some time before noon Kathleen was able to sleep but she was awake again when Graydon first opened his eyes. She turned away. He saw it and knew why. 'How are your eyes this morning?'

'They're bad.'

'Let me see.'

'I tried cold water. I wanted to apply ice, but it had all melted. Anyway, cold doesn't help.'

'I have some Visine in my kit. You want it?'

'Yes.'

'Let me see your eyes.'

She half-turned to him and forced her lids apart. The eyes felt like interior organs surgically exposed.

'Jesus. You look like a god-damned chink.'

'I'll try the Visine.'

'It won't help. You've ruined your looks for the whole weekend. It's just as well we're going back, for I have to say it: I wouldn't take you to a dog fight as long as you look like this. I hope you're not expecting to have breakfast.'

'No.'

'What did I say last night?'

'Don't you remember?'

'I remember most of it.'

'When did you begin to drink like this?'

'I suppose it was seven, eight years ago. When I was living alone.'

'A custom you've never given up.'

'A custom to which I've never become accustomed. That's all. . . . What am I going to do, Kathleen? I love the little boy more than any other human being in the world. Except myself. And my relationship with him has deteriorated so badly these last few months. . . . I love you. I love you very much. But I have two children on my conscience. I'm not about to have three. I would sooner cut Sam into collops and flush him down the toilet than put him through what the twins had to take. That's what's bothering me. what's going to happen to him? I sometimes think now that the girls have taken their troubles and just gone on. I doubt I can do them much more harm. But Sam's troubles are still all to come, whether I stay with Marilyn or not. God, that's terrible to think. Maybe he'll be above it all. I hope so. He's a gutsy little kid.'

In the bathroom Kathleen dripped Visine into her eyes but it only flooded out again, in pale chemical tears that made her cheeks itch. Her lashes were clogged with sticky green matter that looked like snot. She was sure if she took the balls of her eyes between her fingers like two carbuncles and squeezed them putrescence would spatter the glass. Then the lesions would bleed freely and scab and heal, the lanced organs disinfected, the wounds' lips sealed.

She saw Graydon's dark glasses in his kit and put them on. They soothed like bandages. In their medicinal shade her lids knit together. She could see nothing, under the welts of flesh. But sight was safe inside. She would learn to see without light. She would see only herself – only herself, but plainly, as she had never seen plainly anything before. She would see nothing but a woman, fresh and strange and human. Not a beauty. Not a desired object. Not loved and not envied. Nothing but a human being. A person alone. And for a moment she wanted to be like a stone that a sword has pierced. The sword is pulled out and the stone closes. For it seemed terrible to have to see plainly that there are no gods in Olympus. But something else came into her mind, a proverb: 'When you see a blind man, kick him. Why should you be kindlier than God?'

Cade had come to the door, stopping the other side. Looking through the double gloom of the green lenses and the curtained room it seemed to Kathleen she saw a sacred animal there – worshipped, hunted, exterminated nearly. Everything in her mind fell away to the prairie all around Bonnersville, crowded to the horizon with white-headed, round and seedy dandelions blowing to pieces in the wind. A lone bull buffalo the colour of fox, massive, compact on dainty legs, snub-muzzled, louring from the mass of the shoulders, jutting forward from them, not particularly mobile, constrained between the scapulae, in the posture of dejection, facing the earth. 'Oh, we must love the living,' she cried inwardly. 'The living, with all their wounds.' She wished she could tell Graydon how much she loved him. 'I just want to be very good for you,' she said finally, thinking: I didn't know that's what I wanted to be. 'My heart is innocent.'

'I know it is,' he said. 'I know it is.'

'I wish I could tell you how much I love you.'

'I know you do. I know you do,' he said.

Moving to him, saying 'There is enough love, my darling.' Quietly. 'No need to steal any more from the dead.'